THE ARMED FORCES OF THE UNITED KINGDOM
1996-1997

Editor - Charles Heyman

Copyright © R & F (Defence Publications) 1996

ISBN 0 85052 479 2

Price £9.95 (Mail Order £11.45)

Pen & Sword Books Ltd
47 Church Street
Barnsley S70 2AS

Telephone: 01226-734222   Fax: 01226-734438

The Information in this publication has been gathered from unclassified sources.

Front Cover: RAF Harriers on patrol in Turkey. 19 Regiment RA with 105mm Gun and HMS Monmouth on patrol in the Caribbean. Rear Cover: A Battlegroup of 1st (UK) Armoured Division. (Photographs by permission of MOD Public Information).

CONTENTS LIST

Part 4 - The Royal Air Force

Part 5 - The Civilian Sector

Part 6 - Miscellaneous

PART 1 - The MANAGEMENT OF DEFENCE

Government

The executive government of the United Kingdom is vested nominally in the Crown, but for practical purposes in a committee of Ministers that is known as the Cabinet. The head of the ministry and leader of the Cabinet is the Prime Minister. For the implementation of policy the Cabinet is dependent upon the support of a majority of the Members of Parliament in the House of Commons. Within the Cabinet defence matters are the responsibility of the Secretary of State for Defence.

In 1963 the three independent service ministries were merged to form the present Ministry of Defence (MoD). This massive organisation which directly affects the lives of about half a million servicemen, reservists and MoD employed civilians, is controlled by The Secretary of State for Defence who is assisted by two ministers. The first of these is the Minister of State for the Armed Forces and the second the Minister of State for Defence Procurement

The Secretary of State for Defence chairs The Defence Council. This Defence Council is the body that makes the policy decisons that ensure the three services are run efficiently, and in accordance with the wishes of the government of the day.

Defence Roles and Responsibilities

The aim of the United Kingdom's Armed Forces is to deliver and sustain an operational capability wherever and whenever it is required. This overall aim is translated into the three major National Defence Roles:

Defence Role 1 - To ensure the protection and security of the United Kingdom and its dependent territories, even when there is no major external threat.
Defence Role 2 - To ensure against any major external threat to the United Kingdomaf18and its allies.
Defence Role 3 - To contribute towards promoting the United Kingdom's wider security interests through the maintenance of international peace and stability.

These three Defence Roles are further sub-divided into a number of Military Tasks (MT) which accurately define the way in which these MT are actually acomplished.

Total British Armed Forces - Overview (as at 1 April 1995)

Regular: 241,000; Locally Entered 7,200; Regular Reserves 259,600; Volunteer Reserves 71,100; Cadet Forces 135,800; MoD Civilians 142,300

Regular Army 120,000; Royal Navy 51,000; Royal Air Force 70,000; (Note: Royal Naval figure includes some 7,300 Royal Marines and planned redundancies will bring the RAF figure down to 52,500 by "the turn of the century.")

Strategic Forces: 3 x Resolution Class submarines each with 16 x Polaris A-3TK Submarine Launched Ballistic Missiles (SLBM). 1 x Vanguard Class submarine with 16 x Trident D5 SLBM - probably becoming operational in 1995

Navy: 51,000: 12 x Submarines; 3 x Aircraft Carriers; 35 x Destroyers and Frigates; 18 x Mine Counter Measures Vessels; 33 x Patrol Craft; 3 x Harrier Squadrons; 13 x Helicopter Squadrons; 3 x Commando Groups; Royal Fleet Auxiliary - 2 x Large Fleet Tankers; 3 x Small Fleet Tankers; 3 x Support Tankers; 5 x Fleet Replenishment Ships; 1 x Helicopter Support Ship; 5 x Landing Ships; 1 x Forward Repair Ship.

Merchant Naval Vessels Registered in the UK and Crown Dependencies: 106 x Tankers; 22 x Bulk Carriers; 13 x Specialised Carriers; 26 x Cellular Container Ships; 86 x Ro-Ro Passenger and Cargo Ships; 82 x Other General Cargo Ships; 9 x Passenger Ships; 69 x Tugs.

Air Force: 70,000; 6 x Strike/Attack Squadrons; 5 x Offensive Support Squadrons; 6 x Air Defence Squadrons; 3 x Maritime Patrol Squadrons; 5 x Reconnaissance Squadrons; 1 x Airborne Early Warning Squadron; 13 x Transport Squadrons; 3 x Tanker Squadrons; 2 x Search and Rescue Squadrons; 5 x Surface to Air Missile Squadrons; 4 x Ground Defence Squadrons.

Army: 120,000 (including some 5,000 Gurkhas); 1 x Corps Headquarters in

Germany (ARRC); 1 x Armoured Divisional HQ in Germany; 1 x Divisional HQ in UK ; 3 x Brigade Headquarters in Germany; 17 x Brigade Headquarters in UK; 1 x Airborne Brigade in UK ; 1 x Gurkha Infantry Brigade in Hong Kong.

National Police Forces: England and Wales 126,941 Scotland 14,111, Northern Ireland 8,478 (RUC Regular) 4,593 (RUC Reserve)

Defence Council

The composition of The Defence Council is as follows:

The Secretary of State for Defence
Minister of State (Armed Forces)
Minister of State (Defence Procurement)
Parliamentary Under-Secretary of State for the Armed Forces
Chief Scientific Adviser
Chief of Defence Procurement
Chief of Personnel & Logistics
Chief of the Defence Staff
Vice-Chief of the Defence Staff
Chief of the Naval Staff and First Sea Lord
Chief of the Air Staff
Chief of the General Staff
Second Permanent Under Secretary of State

Chief of The Defence Staff

The Chief of the Defence Staff (CDS) is the officer responsible to the Secretary of State for Defence for the co-ordinated effort of all three fighting services. He has his own Central Staff Organisation and has a Vice Chief of the Defence Staff who ranks as number four in the services hierarchy, following the three single service commanders. On 1 January 1996 the Chief of the Defence Staff was:

Field Marshal Sir Peter Inge GCB

Field Marshal Sir Peter Inge was commissioned into the Green Howards from the Royal Military Academy Sandhurst in July 1956.

In 1966, he attended the Staff College at Camberley after which he carried out a staff appointment as a Major in the Ministry of Defence. He completed a course at the Joint Services Defence College in 1971 and then became Brigade Major of 11th Armoured Brigade in Minden.

He was promoted to Lieutenant Colonel in 1972 and joined the Directing Staff at the Staff College at Camberley after which he commanded the 1st Battalion the Green Howards in Chester, Northern Ireland and Berlin from 1974 to 1977. On promotion to Colonel in 1977, he was appointed Commandant of the Junior Division of the Staff College at Warminster.

He commanded 4th Armoured Brigade in Munster in 1979 and became Chief of Staff, Headquarters 1st British Corps in 1982. He was appointed Colonel of the Green Howards in 1982, Colonel Corps of Royal Military Police in 1987 and Colonel Commandant of the Army Physical Training Corps in 1988.

In 1984, he was appointed Commander North East District and 2nd Infantry Division in York. He became Director General of Logistic Policy (Army) at the Ministry of Defence in February 1986 and assumed command of 1st British Corps in August 1987. He was promoted to General and assumed command of Northern Army Group and the British Army of the Rhine on 27 November 1989.

He became Chief of the General Staff in February 1992, before being appointed Chief of the Defence Staff in March 1994. He has served in Hong Kong, Malaya, Libya, West Germany, Northern Ireland and England.

Chain of Command

The Chief of the Defence Staff (CDS) commands and co-ordinates the activities of the three service through the following chain-of-command:

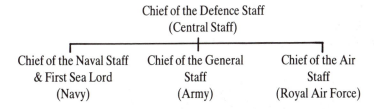

The three single service commanders exercise command of their services through their respective headquarters. However, the complex inter-service nature of the majority of modern military operations, where military, air and naval support must be co-ordinated has led to recent plans for a permanent tri-service Joint Headquarters (JHQ).

Joint Headquarters (JHQ)

The UK MoD has recently announced its intention to set up a permanent JHQ at Northwood in Middlesex. This permanent JHQ should be operational from 1 April 1996 and will replace the previous arrangement, whereby at the onset of a crisis a JHQ was established by a nominated "lead service" and staffed by officers and personnel from the services involved. Staff for the emergency JHQ had to be drafted in from other locations and there were serious disadvantages inherent in this system.

The UK MoD states that "The permanent JHQ will draw together contingency planning, co-ordinate joint operational activities, joint training and exercises, and be a focus for joint doctrine. Concentrated within the permanent JHQ will be those intelligence staff required for the planning and execution of operations. As an organisation, it will therefore be pro-active and anticipatory in its approach to business, monitoring developments in areas of interest to the United Kingdom, and able to conduct planning and devise options for intervention without risk of sending premature political signals. It will also incorporate within it the core of a deployable headquarters, with trained staff who can rapidly and efficiently establish a Joint Force Headquarters in a theatre of operations - as indeed was achieved to great effect last autumn (1995) in response to events in Kuwait."

Operations such as the air defence of the United Kingdom (RAF) and military support to the civil power in Northern Ireland (Army) will continue to remain the responsibility of the single service commands.

Staff Branches

The Staff Branches that you would expect to find at every level in a headquarters from the Ministry of Defence down to garrison/station/port level are as follows:

Commander - The senior officer of the formation who in a large headquarters could be an Admiral, General or Air Marshal. In naval terms the Commander is generally known as the Flag Officer. The Army often refers to the GOC (General Officer Commanding) and the Royal Air Force to the AOC (Air Officer Commanding.

Chief of Staff - The officer who runs the headquarters on a day-to-day basis and who often acts as a second-in-command.

Gl Branch - Responsible for personnel matters including manning,discipline and personal services.

G2 Branch - Responsible for intelligence and security.

G3 Branch - Responsible for operations including staff duties, exercise planning, training, requirements, combat development & tactical doctrine.

G4 Branch - Logistics and quartering.

G5 Branch - Civil and military co-operation.

An operational headquarters in the field will almost certainly be a tri-service organisation with branches from the Army, Navy and Air Force represented. The Staff Branches are the same for all three services.

NATO Command Structure

The United Kingdom is a member of the NATO (North Atlantic Treaty Organisation) and the majority of military operations are conducted in concert with the forces of NATO allies.

Following re-organisations that took effect on 1 July 1993, NATO was reorganised from three into two major Commands. The first is ACLANT (Allied Command Atlantic with headquarters at Norfolk, Virginia (USA) and the second is ACE (Allied Command Europe), with its headquarters at Mons in Belgium.

Operations in the European area in which the United Kingdom was a participant would almost certainly be as part of a NATO force under the command and control of Allied Command Europe (ACE). The current Supreme Allied Commander Europe is General George A Joulwan of the United States Army who replaced General John M Shalikashvili on the 4th of October 1993.

The current organisation of Allied Command Europe is as follows:

Allied Command Europe

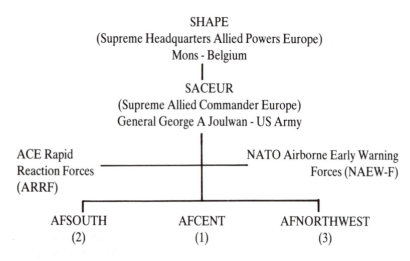

SHAPE
(Supreme Headquarters Allied Powers Europe)
Mons - Belgium

SACEUR
(Supreme Allied Commander Europe)
General George A Joulwan - US Army

ACE Rapid Reaction Forces (ARRF)

NATO Airborne Early Warning Forces (NAEW-F)

AFSOUTH (2)   AFCENT (1)   AFNORTHWEST (3)

Notes:

(1) AFCENT - Allied Forces Central European Theatre with headquartes at Brunssum in the Netherlands and with overall responsibility for military operations in Central Europe. AFCENT is further subdivided into three subordinate commands - see next diagram.

(2) AFSOUTH - Allied Forces Southern Europe, with headquarters at Naples in Italy and responsible for military operations in the area of Turkey, Greece and Italy.

(3) AFNORTHWEST - Allied Forces North-western Europe, with headquarters at High Wycombe in the UK. This new headquarters, was operational as from 1 July 1994 and is responsible for operations in Norway, the UK, and the maritime area between the two countries. The Chief of Staff is Lieutenant General Ola Aabakken of the Norwegian Army.

HQ AFNORTHWEST claims to be leaner and more efficient than its predecessor AFNORTH at Oslo in Norway. The headquaters is staffed by about 300 personnel, the majority of which are British, American and Norwegians, but Belgium, Canada, Denmark, Germany and the Netherlands are all represented.

Following re-organisation the composition of AFCENT is as follows:

Allied Forces Central European Theatre

AFCENT
Commander-in-Chief
Allied Forces Central Europe
(CINCENT)
General H von Ondarza
German Army
HQ Brunssum - Netherlands

AIRCENT (1)	LANDCENT	BALTAP
Commander	Commander	Commander
Allied Air Forces	Allied Land Forces	Allied Forces Baltic
Central Europe	Central Europe	Approaches
General RB Oaks USAF	General MJ Wilmink	Lt General KGH Hillingsoe
HQ Ramstein - Germany	Netherlands Army	Danish Army
	HQ Heidelberg - Germany	HQ Karup - Denmark

Note:

(1) AIRCENT is now responsible for all air forces in the AFCENT region
(2) The AFCENT operational area now includes Northern Germany and Denmark, extending 800 kms to the south to the Swiss and Austrian borders.

The Allied Rapid Reaction Corps (ARRC)

Operations on the European mainland will most probably be in support of the ARRC. This formation is the land component of the Allied Command Europe Rapid Reaction Forces and it will be prepared for employment in support of SACEUR'S crisis management options whenever necessary. Its peacetime planning structure includes 10 divisions, plus corps troops from 12 NATO nations to allow a rapid response to a wide range of eventualities.

The ARRC will consist of:

a. National divisions from Germany, the United Kingdom and the United States; Spain will also provide a division under special co-ordination agreements

b. The Multinational Division central (MND-C), which will include Belgian, German, Dutch and British airmobile units.

c. The Multinational Division south (MND-S), which will include Greek, Italian and Turkish units.

d. Two framework divisions under the lead of one nation: one of these is British with an Italian component and the other Italian with a Portuguese component. Greece and Turkey have each assigned a division with the potential to framework with another nation.

The operational organisation, composition and size of the ARRC would depend on the type of crisis, area of crisis, its political significance, and the capabilities and availability of lift assets, the distances to be covered and the infrastructure capabilities of the nation receiving assistance. It is considered that a four-division ARRC would be the maximum employment structure.

The headquarters of the ARRC is multinational. It is temporarily located at Bielefeld in Germany, but in the future will be located in Rheindahlen.

In peace, the headquarters of the ARRC and the two Multinational Divisions are under the command and control of SACEUR, but the remaining divisions and units only come under SACEUR's operational control after being deployed. The ARRC was activated in October 1992, but the corps itself only became operational in 1995. The commander of the ARRC is a British Lt General.

The main British contribution to the ARRC is 1 (UK) Armoured Division that is stationed in Germany and a considerable number of British personnel in both the ARRC Corps HQ and Corps Troops. In addition, in times of tension 3(UK) Div and 24 Airmobile Bde will move to the European mainland to take their place in the ARRC's order of battle. In total, we believe that some 55,000 British Regular soldiers could be assigned to the ARRC (23,000 resident in Germany) together with a substantial numbers of Regular Army Reservists and formed TA Units.

The mission statement of the ARRC is as follows:

"Be prepared to deploy ARRC forces of corps troops and up to four divisions on military operations in support of SACEUR's crisis management options"

Outline Composition of the ARRC (ACE Rapid Reaction Corps)

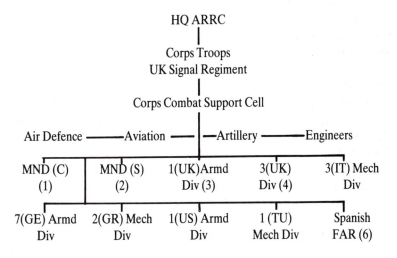

Notes: (1) MND(C) - Multinational Division - Central; (2) Multinational Division - South (3) Resident in Germany (4) Resident in the UK.

(5) IT - Italy; GE - Germany; GR - Greece; TU - Turkey (6) FAR - Rapid Action Force.

Further details on the UK Army components of the ARRC are given in Part 3 and a complete breakdown of the international contributions to the ARRC is contained in Part 6.

The Finances of Defence

> "You need three things to win a war,
> Money, money and more money."
> Trivulzio (1441-1518)

In general terms defence is related to money, and a nation's ability to pay for its defence is linked to its GDP (Gross Domestic Product) as measured by the sum of all economic activity within a country. Estimates for the world's top six GDP rankings for 1994-95 (in billions of US$) are as follows:

United States	-	$5,905 billion
Japan	-	$3,508 billion
Germany	-	$1,846 billion
France	-	$1,279 billion
Italy	-	$1,187 billion
United Kingdom	-	$1,025 billion

For comparison purposes defence expenditure is often expressed as a percentage of GDP.

The UK Government plans to spend the following amounts on defence (cash provision) during the next two years:-

| 1996-97 | - | 21.92 billion pounds |
| 1997-98 | - | 22.31 billion pounds |

Overall Defence Expenditure is expected to fall by about 11% in real terms between 1992-93 and 1997-98, with defence spending representing approximately 3.8% of GDP (Gross Domestic Product) in 1992-93 and declining to about 2.8% of GDP in 1997-98. In 1985 Defence Expenditure represented 5.2% of GDP

A reasonable illustration of the changes in UK Defence Expenditure are a comparison of defence spending totals that have been rounded/adjusted to 1993-94 prices:

1970-71	-	16.46 billion
1975-76	-	22.19 billion
1980-81	-	23.79 billion
1985-86	-	27.84 billion
1990-91	-	25.45 billion
1995-96	-	21.72 billion (planned)

The total Central Government Expenditure plans for the FY 1995-96 are budgeted at 305 billion and for comparison purposes the Government's major expenditure programmes during FY 1995-96 are as follows:

Defence	21.72	billion
Overseas Aid	2.36	billion
Health	32.96	billion
Transport	4.39	billion
Housing	6.90	billion
Home Office	6.41	billion
Education	10.96	billion
Social Security	87.07	billion
Agriculture	3.02	billion
Employment	3.46	billion
Legal Departments	2.80	billion
Local Government	30.29	billion
Scotland	14.11	billion
Wales	6.63	billion
Northern Ireland	7.30	billion
Debt Interest	24.50	billion
Miscellaneous	40.12	billion

Defence Budgets - NATO Comparison

The nations of the North Atlantic Treaty Organisation (NATO), of which the United Kingdom is a member state, spent some US$418.5 billion on defence during 1994. For ease of conversions from national currencies amounts are shown in US$:

NATO Defence Expenditure 1994	-	US$464.6 billion
NATO (European Nations) Defence Expenditure 1994	-	US$171.9 billion

The next table shows the defence budget for each NATO nation during 1994 with figures in brackets representing defence expenditure as percentage of GDP

USA	-	US$ 283.1 billion (4.%)
France	-	U$ 44.38 billion(3.4%)
Germany	-	US$ 35.9 billion (1.8%)
UK	-	US$ 34.06 billion (3.3%)
Italy	-	US$ 21.19 billion (2.1%)
Canada	-	US$ 9.52 billion (1.8%)
Spain	-	US$ 7.61 billion (1.6%)
Netherlands	-	US$ 7.09 billion (2.2%)
Turkey	-	US$ 4.92 billion (4.1%)
Greece	-	US$ 4.34 billion (5.6%)
Belgium	-	US$ 3.94 billion (1.8%)
Norway	-	US$ 3.42 billion (3.2%)
Denmark	-	US$ 2.74 billion (1.9%)
Portugal	-	US$ 2.28 billion (3.0%)
Luxembourg	-	US$ 124 million (1.1%)

Note: Iceland has no military expenditure although it remains a member of NATO.

An interesting comparison is made by the total national defence budget divided by the total number of full time personnel in all three services.

Figures for the top five world defence spending nations are as follows:-

Ranking	Nation	1994 Defence Budget	Total Service Personnel	Cost Per Serviceman
1	USA	US$283.1 bn	1,650,500	US$171,623
2	Japan	US$44.4 bn	237,700	US$186,790
3	France	US$44.3 bn	409,600	US$108,154
4	Germany	US$35.9 bn	367,300	US$97,740
5	UK	US$34.0 bn	254,300	US$133,700

Note: Russia should probably be the second nation in this table, but because of the effects of inflation it is currently impossible to make a meaningful conversion from Roubles to US$. Problems in October 1994 when the rouble fell from around 1,800 to 3,000 to the US Dollar have made the problem worse. Most defence analysts are using a figure of US$30 billion as the Russian 1994 defence budget.

UK Defence Budget - Top Level Budget Holders

Under the early 1990s "New Management Strategy" the Defence Budget was allocated to a series of "Top Level Budget Holders" each of whom were allocated a budget with which to run their departments. The money allocated to these Top Level Budgets (TLBs) constitutes the building bricks upon which the whole of the defence budget is based.

Top Level Budgets 1995-1996

Naval Operational Areas (C-in-C Fleet)	£1,165.9	million
Army Operational Areas (C-in-C Land Command)	£2,828.6	million
Air Force Operational Areas (AOC RAF Strike Command)	£1,688.6	million
Overseas Garrisons (Vice Chief of the Defence Staff)	£361.5	million
Service Personnel		
2nd Sea Lord (Navy)	£693.4	million
Adjutant General (Army) Personnel & Training	£1,001.2	million

AOC RAF Personnel & Training Command	£798.4	million
Logistics, Support & Maintenance		
Chief of Fleet Support	£2,019.5	million
Quartermaster General	£1,121.7	million
AOC RAF Logistics Command	£1,816.8	million
MOD Headquarters & Centrally Managed Expenditure	£658.8	million
Vice Chief of the Defence Staff (Headquarters)	£817.8	million
Chief of Defence Procurement	£1,017.6	million
Equipment		
Sea Systems	£1,209.4	million
Land Systems	£1,311.0	million
Air Systems	£2,101.0	million
Meteorological Office	£80.4	million
Defence Evaluation and Research Agency	£506.3	million
Non Budgetary Major Research Expenditure	£462,4	million
Loans & Grants	£43,9	million
Total Budget 1995-96	**£21,720 million**	

In percentage terms the breakdown of the 1995-96 Defence Budget figure of £21.72 billion pounds can be shown for all three services as follows:

Equipment Purchases	-	40.0%
Service Personnel	-	28.0%
Civilian Personel	-	12.0%
Works & Miscellaneus Services	-	20.0%

Equipment Expenditure

The equipment expenditure figure can be broken down further, to reveal that during the 1995-96 Financial Year a total of £9.01 billion will be spent, with money going to the services as follows:

Sea Systems	-	£2.203 billion
Land Systems	-	£1.841 billion
Air Systems	-	£3.357 billion
Other	-	£1.618 billion

Note: In general Sea, Land and Air Systems relate to Naval, Army and Air Force expenditure. Overall some 79% of the equipment budget relates to UK expenditure, 12% on collaborative expenditure and 9% on overseas expenditure

Some of the more interesting equipment expenditure figures for the 1995-96 Financial Year (the latest year for which the figures are available) are amongst the following:

Navy

Ships, Hulls and Machinery	-	£421 million
Weapon Systems	-	£367 million
Ship Equipment & Support Services	-	£177 million
Ship/Weapon Maintenance Stores & Equip	-	£602 million
Dockyard Services	-	£433 million

Army

Guns, Small Arms and NBC Defence Stores	-	£51 million
Ammunition, Mines and Explosives	-	£126 million
Armoured Fighting Vehicles	-	£231 million
Load Carrying Vehicles	-	£214 million
Engineering Equipment	-	£68 million
Guided Weapons	-	£245 million
Communications	-	£223 million
Surveillance Equipment	-	£78 million
Maintenance	-	£378 million
Air Force Aircraft, Engines & Aircraft Equipment	-	£1,528 million
Guided Weapons & Electronic Equipment	-	£1,182 million

Reserve Forces

In an emergency the UK MoD could call upon a tri-service reserve component of some 327,600 personnel (mid 1995 figure). This figure is composed of Regular Reserves and Volunteer Forces. Regular Reserves (262,900) comprise ex-service personnel who have completed regular service and have a reserve liability in civilian life. The Volunteer Forces (64,700) comprise volunteers who may not have had prior regular service and train on a part time basis, generally at establishments close to their home. During mid 1995 the Reserve Forces totals were as follows:

	Regular Reserves	Volunteer Forces
Royal Navy & Royal Marines	22,100	3,700
Army	195,300	59,700
Royal Air Force	45,500	1,300

During mid 1995 and to allow for discussion amongst interested parties the MoD published the draft of the new Reserve Forces Bill before its submission to Parliament. The new legislation (last updated in 1966) seeks to allow for more flexibility in calling out reserves, and should enable qualified reservists to volunteer for peacetime service in areas such as Bosnia or the Falklands without putting their civilian employment at risk.

The bill suggests a new category of "sponsored reserves" with personnel working for a unit/civilian firm in the UK on the understanding that they will become uniformed personnel and travel overseas, if the unit they are supporting suddenly goes off to support, for example a UN type operation in Bosnia or Angola. Another category of about 3,000 specialists will be created to allow people with vital skills to be called up more quickly.

First reactions to the plans appear to be favourable.

Defence Personnel Totals

Total Service and Civilian Personnel Strength (1 April 1995)

UK Service Personnel	233,300
UK Civilian Personnel	116,100
Locally Entered/Engaged Service Personnel	5,200

Locally Entered/Engaged Civilian Personnel	16,900
Royal Irish (Home Service)	5,300
	376,800

Strength of UK Regular Forces (1 April 1995)

Royal Navy	Officers	Other Ranks
Trained	7,700	40,500
Untrained	1,100	1,600
Army	Officers	Other Ranks
Trained	13,100	91,500
Untrained	900	6,300
Royal Air Force	Officers	Other Ranks
Trained	11,800	57, 600
Untrained	1,000	300

Deployment in Operational Areas (1 April 1995)

C-in-C Fleet (Royal Navy)	Officers	Other Ranks
Naval Aviation	1,000	4,800
Fleet Infrastructure	400	1,800
Surface Fleet	1,000	10,000
Submarines	500	3,300
Minor War Vessels	200	1,200
Royal Marines	700	6,100
	3,800	**27,200**

C-in-C Land Command (Army)	Officers	Other Ranks
Scotland	200	1,500
2nd Division	700	8,000
London District	300	3,900
4th Division	1,200	14,200
5th Division	300	3,200
1st (UK) Armoured Division	1,300	18,000
UK Support Command (Germany)	700	3,600

3rd UK Division	600	7,500
GOC Northern Ireland	800	9,700
Administration	1,000	2,800
	7,200	**72,400**

AOC-in-C Strike Command (RAF)	Officers	Other Ranks
1 Group - Strike/Attack (UK)	1,100	9,700
38 Group - Air Movements	1,000	6,200
11 Group - Air Defence	1,100	8,600
18 Group - Maritime & SAR	800	5,800
2 Group - Strike/Attack (BFG)	600	4,700
HQ & Administrative Support	900	2,100
	5,600	**37,100**

Overseas Deployment (1 April 1995)

Continental Europe
Royal Navy/Royal Marines	1,310
Army	26,465
Royal Air Force	5,974
Civilians	1,431

Gibraltar
Royal Navy/Royal Marines	407
Army	65
Royal Air Force	154
Civilians	80

Cyprus
Royal Navy/Royal Marines	2
Army	2,873
Royal Air Force	1,441
Civilians	236

Other Mediterranean, Gulf & Near East
Royal Navy/Royal Marines	2,009
Army	191
Royal Air Force	364
Civilians	6

Hong Kong

Royal Navy/Royal Marines	185
Army	514
Royal Air Force	208
Civilians	94

Other Far East

Royal Navy/Royal Marines	43
Army	201
Royal Air Force	24
Civilians	26

Other Locations

Royal Navy/Royal Marines	1,567
Army	2,869
Royal Air Force	1,728
Civilians	2,536

Note: These tables include personnel on detachment from units in the UK and the final list (Other Locations) includes personnel on detachment to the Falkland Islands.

Recruitment of UK Regular Forces (1994-1995)

	Officers	Other Ranks
Royal Navy	166 (665)	1,135 (4,704)
Army	823 (1,525)	9,861 (18,743)
Royal Air Force	216 (936)	806 (6,078)

For Comparison - 1985-86 figures are in brackets

Outflow of UK Regular Forces (1994-1995)

	Officers	Other Ranks
Royal Navy	667 (771)	5,518 (7,232)
Army	1,943 (1,985)	19,942 (19,316)
Royal Air Force	962 (983)	5,008 (6,234)

For Comparison - 1985-86 figures are in brackets. The 1994-95 figures include all those who left the services on redundancy.

PART 2 - THE ROYAL NAVY

Royal Naval Summary:

Strategic Forces: 2 x Resolution Class submarines each with 16 x Polaris A- 3TK Submarine Launched Ballistic Missiles (SLBM). 2 x Vanguard Class Submarines each equipped with 16 x Trident D5 SLBM (2 more building).

12 x Fleet Submarines; 3 x Aircraft Carriers; 36 x Destroyers and Frigates; 18 x Mine Counter Measures Vessels; 32 x Patrol Craft; 4 x Harrier Squadrons; 13 x Helicopter Squadrons; 3 x Commando Groups: Royal Fleet Auxiliary - 2 x Large Fleet Tankers; 3 x Small Fleet Tankers; 4 x Support Tankers; 5 x Fleet Replenishment Ships; 1 x Aviation Training Ship; 5 x Landing Ships; 1 x Forward Repair Ship.

The total personnel strength of the Royal Navy at 1 April 1995 was:

Officers	8,800	(1,100)
Other Ranks	42,100	(1,600)
	50,900	**(2,700)**

Figures in brackets relate to personel undergoing basic training.

Composition of the Fleet

Submarines

Trident	2	Vanguard, Victorious.	Faslane
Polaris	2	Repulse, Renown.	Faslane
Fleet	7	Tireless, Torbay, Trafalgar. Turbulent, Trenchant, Talent. Triumph.	Devonport
	5	Sceptre, Spartan, Splendid. Superb, Sovereign.	Faslane

ASW Carriers

| | 3 | Invincible, Illustrious, Ark Royal. | Portsmouth |

Destroyers

| **(Type 42)** | 12 | Cardiff, Exeter, Manchester, Newcastle, Nottingham, Southampton, Glasgow, Liverpool, York, Gloucester, Birmingham, Edinburgh. | Portsmouth |

Frigates

| **(Type 23)** | 10 | Norfolk, Marlborough, Iron Duke, Monmouth, Montrose, Westminster, Northumberland, Somerset, Argyll, Lancaster. | Devonport |
| | 1 | Richmond. | Portsmouth |

Frigates

| **(Type 22)** | 13 | Battleaxe, Beaver, Boxer, Brazen Brilliant, Brave, Campbeltown, Chatham, Cornwall, London, Coventry, Cumberland, Sheffield | Devonport |

(Broadsword, Battleaxe, Brilliant and Brazen will be sold to the Brazilian Navy between 1996 and 1997)

| **Assault Ships** | 2 | Fearless, Intrepid. | Portsmouth |

Offshore Patrol

| **(Castle Class)** | 2 | Dumbarton Castle, Leeds Castle. | Faslane/ Portsmouth |
| **(Island Class)** | 6 | Alderney, Gurnsey, Anglesey, Lindisfarne, Orkney, Shetland. | Faslane/ Portsmouth |

Minehunters

| **(Hunt Class)** | 7 | Berkley, Brocklesby, Chiddingford, | Faslane/ |

		Dulverton, Ledbury, Middleton, Quorn.	Portsmouth
	6	Atherstone, Cattistock, Cottesmore, Hurworth, Brecon, Bicester.	Portsmouth
(Sandown Class)	5	Sandown, Inverness, Cromer, Walney, Bridport.	Faslane/ Portsmouth
Patrol Craft			
(Peacock Class)	3	Peacock, Plover, Starling	Hong Kong
(River Class)	4	Blackwater, Itchen, Spey, Arun	Faslane/
	1	Orwell.	Portsmouth
Costal Training Craft	14	Biter, Blazer, Archer, Charger, Dasher, Smiter, Puncher, Pursuer, Example, Explorer, Express, Exploit, Loyal Watcher, Loyal Chancellor.	

(These 14 vessels are operated by Royal Naval University Training Units)

Search & Rescue Craft	2	Ranger, Trumpeter.	Gibraltar
Support Ships			
Royal Yacht	1	Britannia.	Portsmouth
Ice Patrol	1	Endurance.	Portsmouth
Survey Ships	4	Beagle, Herald, Hecla Bulldog, Roebuck	Devonport
	1	Gleaner.	Portsmouth

Note: Not all of these ships will be available for operations at any one time and there will always be ships in refit or engaged on trials or training. One of the ASW Carriers is generally in refit (during 1995 HMS Ark Royal) and on average 5-7 destroyers/frigates from a total force of 36 will be in refit/standby.

Royal Fleet Auxiliary

Large Fleet Tankers	2	Olna, Olwen.
Small Fleet Tankers	3	Black Rover, Gold Rover, Grey Rover.
Support Tankers	4	Bayleaf, Brambleaf, Oakleaf, Orangeleaf.
Replenishment Ships	5	Fort George, Fort Austin, Fort Grange Resource, Fort Victoria.
Aviation Training Ship	1	Argus.
Landing Ship	5	Sir Galahad, Sir Geraint, Sir Bedivere, Sir Percivale, Sir Tristram.
Forward Repair Ship	1	Diligence

Fleet Air Arm

Air Defence	Sea Harrier FRS1, F/A2	6	800 Sqn
Recce/Attack	Sea Harrier FRS1, F/A2F/A2	6	801 Sqn
Sea Harrier	FRS1, F/A2	6	899 Sqn
Harrier	T4	4	899 Sqn
Anti-Submarine	Sea King HAS 5/6	13	810 Sqn
Sea King	HAS 5/6	7	814 Sqn
Sea King	HAS 5/6	9	819 Sqn
Sea King	HAS 5/6	7	820 Sqn
Sea King	HAS 5/6	11	706 Sqn

Anti-Submarine/	Lynx HAS 3, HMA 8	38	815 Sqn
Anti-Ship	Lynx HAS 3, HMA 8	12	702 Sqn
Airborne Early Warning	Sea King AEW 29	8	49 Sqn
Commando Assault	Sea King HC4	8	845 Sqn
Sea King	HC4	8	846 Sqn
Sea King	HC4	8	848 Sqn
Aircrew Training	Gazelle HT2	17	705 Sqn
	Jetstream T2	13	750 Sqn
Fleet Support/	Sea King Mk5	5	771 Sqn
Search & Rescue	Sea King Mk4	5	772 Sqn
Fleet Training	Hawk	12	
& Support	Jetstream T3	3	

Note: Aircraft on charge to 815, 702 and 849 Sqns are deployed in flights of single or multiple aircraft

Royal Marines
1 x Commando Brigade Headquarters
1 x Brigade Air Squadron
3 x Royal Marine Commando (Battalion Size)
1 x Commando Regiment Royal Artillery
1 x Commando Artillery Battery (Volunteer)
1 x Commando Squadron Royal Engineers
1 x Commando Squadron Royal Engineers (Volunteer)
1 x Commando Logistic Regiment
1 x Special Boat Service Squadrons
2 x Assault Squadrons (Landing Craft)
1 x Security Unit for National Strategic Deterrent

The Merchant Navy

Merchant Naval Vessels Registered in the UK and Crown Dependencies: 106 x Tankers (2161); 22 x Bulk Carriers (293); 13 x Specialised Carriers (124) ; 26 x Cellular Container Ships (1017); 86 x Ro-Ro Passenger and Cargo Ships (657) ; 82 x Other General Cargo Ships (145); 9 x Passenger Ships (272); 69 x Tugs

Note: This listing refers to vessels of 500 gross tons and over. The figures in brackets refer to thousands of gross tons relating to each type of vessel. The total is 4,670 thousand gross tons

The Admiralty Board

The routine management of the Royal Navy is the responsibility of The Admiralty Board the composition of which is as follows:

The Secretary of State for Defence
Minister of State (Armed Forces)
Minister of State (Defence Procurement)
Parliamentary Under-Secretary of State for Defence
Chief of the Naval Staff and First Sea Lord
Commander in Chief Fleet
Second Sea Lord and Commander in Chief Naval Home Command
Second Permanent Under Secretary of State and Secretary of the Admiralty Board
Chief of Fleet Support
Controller of the Navy
Assistant Chief of Naval Staff

Decisions made by The Defence Council or the Admiralty Board are acted upon by the naval staff at the various headquarters throughout the defence chain-of-command. The First Sea Lord is the officer responsible for the Royal Navy's contribution to the national defence effort and he maintains control through the commander and the staff branches of each of these headquarters.

First Sea Lord and Chief of the Naval Staff
Admiral Sir Jock Slater GCB, LVO, ADC

Admiral Sir Jock Slater became the First Sea Lord and Chief of the Naval Staff in July 1995. He was born in Edinburgh in 1938 and educated at the Edinburgh Academy and Sedbergh. He entered the Royal Naval College, Dartmouth, in

1956 passing out in 1958 with the Sword of Honour and a Queen's Telescope.

As a Sub Lieutenant, he served in the frigate HMS TROUBRIDGE in the West Indies and as First Lieutenant of the trials minesweeper HMS YAXHAM, at Portland.

As a Lieutenant, Admiral Slater served in HMY BRITANNIA (1961-62), the destroyer HMS CASSANDRA in the Far East (1962-63) and commanded the minesweeper HMS SOBERTON on UK Fishery Protection duties in 1965. After qualifying as a Navigation Specialist, he served in the aircraft carrier HMS VICTORIOUS in the Far East (1966-67) and as a Squadron Navigating Officer of the Dartmouth Training Squadron in HMS SCARBOROUGH (1967-68).

Admiral Slater became Equerry to HM The Queen in 1968 and held this appointment until 1971 when he was promoted to Commander and took command of the Leander Class frigate HMS JUPITER (1972-73). He subsequently spent two years in the Directorate of Naval operations in the Ministry of Defence. He was promoted to Captain in 1976 and commanded the guided missile destroyer HMS KENT (1976-77) followed by a year at the Royal College of Defence Studies in London. He returned to the Naval Staff in 1979 as Assistant Director of Naval Warfare. In 1982 he became the first Captain of the aircraft carrier HMS ILLUSTRIOUS. He subsequently commanded the School of Maritime Operations at HMS DRYAD (1983-85).

He was promoted to Rear Admiral in 1985 and became Assistant Chief of the Defence Staff, responsible for Policy and Nuclear affairs in the Ministry of Defence in London. In 1987 he was promoted Vice Admiral and became Flag Officer Scotland and Northern Ireland and Naval Base Commander, Rosyth; he also held the NATO appointments of Commander Northern Sub Area Eastern Atlantic and Commander NORE Sub Area Channel. In 1989 he became Chief of Fleet Support.

In early 1991 he was promoted to Admiral and became the Commander-in-Chief Fleet and the Allied Commander-in-Chief Channel and Eastern Atlantic.
Before assuming his present appointment he was appointed Vice Chief of the Defence Staff in 1993.

Royal Naval Chain of Command

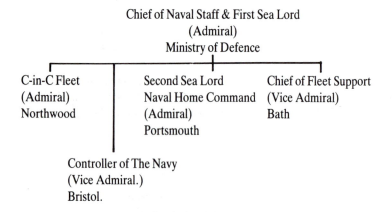

Chief of Naval Staff & First Sea Lord
(Admiral)
Ministry of Defence

C-in-C Fleet
(Admiral)
Northwood

Second Sea Lord
Naval Home Command
(Admiral)
Portsmouth

Chief of Fleet Support
(Vice Admiral)
Bath

Controller of The Navy
(Vice Admiral.)
Bristol.

Commander-in-Chief Fleet

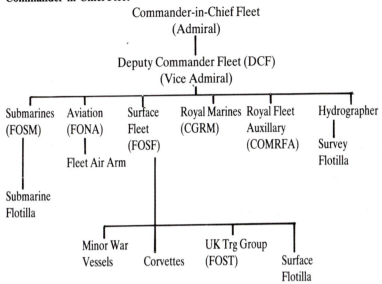

Notes: FOSM - Flag Officer Submarines; FONA - Flag Officer Naval Aviation; FOSF - Flag Officer Surface Fleet; CGRM - Commandant General Royal Marines; COMRFA - Commander Royal Fleet Auxillary; FOST - Flag Officer Sea Training

Naval Home Command

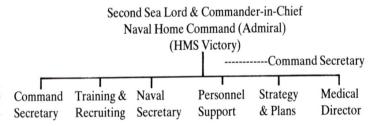

Chief of Fleet Support

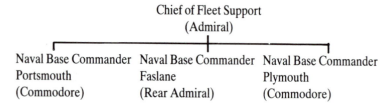

Chief of Fleet Support
(Admiral)

Naval Base Commander Portsmouth (Commodore)	Naval Base Commander Faslane (Rear Admiral)	Naval Base Commander Plymouth (Commodore)

Fleet Disposition

Submarine Flotilla

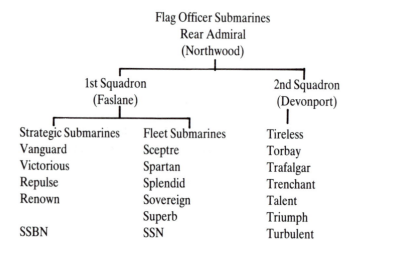

Flag Officer Submarines
Rear Admiral
(Northwood)

1st Squadron
(Faslane)

2nd Squadron
(Devonport)

Strategic Submarines	Fleet Submarines	Tireless
Vanguard	Sceptre	Torbay
Victorious	Spartan	Trafalgar
Repulse	Splendid	Trenchant
Renown	Sovereign	Talent
	Superb	Triumph
SSBN	SSN	Turbulent

Surface Flotilla

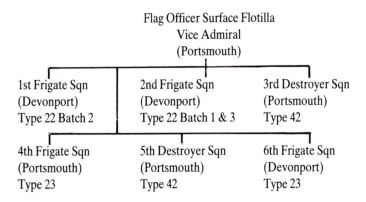

Flag Officer Surface Flotilla
Vice Admiral
(Portsmouth)

1st Frigate Sqn	2nd Frigate Sqn	3rd Destroyer Sqn
(Devonport)	(Devonport)	(Portsmouth)
Type 22 Batch 2	Type 22 Batch 1 & 3	Type 42

4th Frigate Sqn	5th Destroyer Sqn	6th Frigate Sqn
(Portsmouth)	(Portsmouth)	(Devonport)
Type 23	Type 42	Type 23

Mine Counter Measures Flotilla

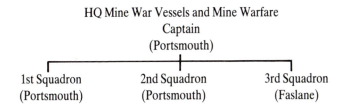

HQ Mine War Vessels and Mine Warfare
Captain
(Portsmouth)

1st Squadron	2nd Squadron	3rd Squadron
(Portsmouth)	(Portsmouth)	(Faslane)

Surveying Flotilla - Headquarters at Devonport

Outline Organisation of a Frigate

The organisation of a typical RN frigate is the result of hundreds of years of evolution and above all, the ship is organised to fight. The four major departments in a modern frigate are the following:

33

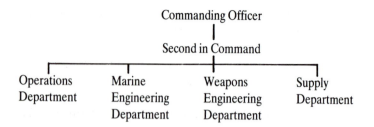

Operations Department - This department basically "fights" the ship and is the direct descendant of the Seaman Branch who manned the guns in earlier generations. There is usually a helicopter embarked and the flight commander reports to the Head of the Operations Department.

Marine Engineering Department - Runs the machinery of the ship ie. the main propulsion units that drive the vessel (gas turbines or diesels), the electrical power supplies and all of the ancillary machinery required.

Weapons Engineering Department - Responsible for the efficient functioning of all of the ship's highly complex sensors and weapons.

Supply Department - Responsible for the logistic arrangements in the ship ie. catering, spares for all of the weapons, general stores, sensors and machinery spares and for all pay and accounting matters.

All of the departments are inter-dependent and each has a head of department - known collectively as "the HODs". These HODs meet at regular intervals and agree such matters as programmes, training and the efficient administration of everything on board. Whilst each HOD is responsible directly to the commanding officer for the efficiency of his department, the Head of the Operations Department generally leads the HODs and is the Second-in-Command - he is known as the First Lieutenant and is a Lieutenant Commander. The other HODs are also likely to be Lieutenant Commanders and, even if senior to the First Lieutenant, are subordinate to him - the First Lieutenant is the man who takes over if the Commanding Officer is unable to perform his duties.

The cleaning of the ship and all of the general tasks are shared by the departments and the HODs would discuss these matters at their meetings - for example, they would agree how many sailors would be required from each department for a storing at sea operation. A recent development is the presence on board many RN ships of female personnel. These females share all of the duties of their male counterparts but, of course, have separate living quarters.

The Commanding Officer is usually a Commander RN (with a background in the Operations Department) and he is known as "The Captain". In command of a squadron of frigates you will find an officer with the rank of Captain RN who doubles the duties both of "Captain" of his ship and Captain (F) to whom the "Captains" of the frigates in his squadron report.

The complement of a frigate relates to the requirement to man the ship for battle. A Batch 3 Type 22 has a total of 232 (13 officers) and a newer Duke Class Type 23 has a complement of 169 (12 officers).

Royal Naval Shore Establishments

HMS Cambridge	Plymouth	Gunnery (closure April 1996)
HMS Cochrane	Rosyth	Naval Base
HMS Collingwood	Fareham	Weapons Engineering
HMS Daedalus	Lee-on-Solent	Air Engineering & RNAS (closure April 1996)
Dartmouth BRNC	Dartmouth	Officer Training
HMS Dolphin	Gosport	Submarine Training
HMS Drake	Devonport	Naval Base
HMS Dryad	Fareham	Maritime Operations School
HMS Forest Moor	Harrogate	Communications Base
HMS Gannet	Prestwick	RN Air Station
HMS Heron	Yeovilton	RN Air Station
HMS Nelson	Portsmouth	Naval Base
HMS Neptune	Faslane	Naval Base
HMS Osprey	Portland	RN Air Station (closes 1999)
HMS Raleigh	Torpoint	Training Base
HMS Seahawk	Helston	RNAS Culdrose
HMS Sultan	Gosport	Marine Engineering
HMS Tamar	Hong Kong	Naval Base

HMS Victory	Portsmouth	C-in-C Home Command
HMS Warrior	Northwood	C-in-C Fleet
HMS Excellent	Portsmouth	Operations and Training

Royal Naval Reserve Units

There are Royal Naval Reserve Units located at:

HMS Calliope	Gateshead
HMS Cambria	Penarth
HMS Caroline	Northern Ireland
HMS Dalriada	Greenock
HMS Eaglet	Liverpool
HMS Flying Fox	Bristol
HMS Forward	Birmingham
HMS Northwood	Northwood
HMS President	London
HMS Scotia	Pitreavie
HMS Sherwood	Nottingham
HMS Vivid	Devonport
HMS King Alfred	Portsmouth
HMS Ferret	Ashford

Strategic Deterrent

The United Kingdom's Strategic Deterrent is operated by the Royal Navy and submarine launched ballistic missiles (SLBM) have been installed in Royal Naval submarines since the late 1960s, with operational patrols commencing in 1969. The first class of SSBN (Nuclear Powered Ballistic Missile Submarine) was the Resolution Class with 4 x vessels of the type:

HMS Resolution	(Commissioned 1967)
HMS Repulse	(Commissioned 1968)
HMS Renown	(Commissioned 1968)
HMS Revenge	(Commissioned 1969)

Resolution Class submarines carried the Polaris 3-TK missile, armed with 6 x 150 kT MRV (Multiple Re-entry Vehicle) warheads. The 3-TK system is believed to have a range of approximately 4,500 kms.

The Resolution Class SSBN are in the process of being replaced by the Vanguard Class, and HMS Vanguard the lead vessel of the class is believed to have commenced its first patrol in late 1994/early 1995. The Trident Class submarines of which there will be four, are armed with 16 x US Trident II D5 missiles and each missile has the capability of carrying up to 12 MIRV (Multiple Independently Targeted Re-entry Vehicle) warheads making a possible total of 192 warheads per submarine. However, in late 1994 the UK MoD announced that HMS Vanguard would only deploy with a total of 96 UK designed and built A-90 warheads and in general terms, we believe that in UK service the Trident II D5 will carry eight warheads per missile.

The UK is believed to have purchased 67 x Trident 2D-5 missiles from the United States and the range of the missile is believed to be in excess of 9,000 kms with a CEP (Circular Error Probable) of about 100 metres.

The second vessel in the class HMS Victorious should be ready for operational deployment by the end of 1995 and the third vessel HMS Vigilant being ready for operational deployment by the end of 1996. UK MoD delay in placing the order for the fourth and final vessel of the class (HMS Vengance) means that this submarine will probably not be ready for operational deployment until 1998. To cover this gap two Polaris submarines, HMS Repulse and HMS Renown will be retained in service with the last Polaris submarine expected to "pay off" when HMS Vengance becomes operational.

Plans are for at least one of these SSBN to be on patrol constantly and because of their high speed, long endurance underwater, and advanced sensor and electronic equipment, they have little fear of detection

These large submarines displace over 16,000 tonnes, have a length of 150 metres and the three decks offer accommodation for the crew of 130 which is unusually spacious for a submarine. Good domestic facilities are provided for the crew and the air purification system enables them to remain submerged for long periods without any outside support. Each submarine has two crews known as Port and Starboard; when one crew is away on patrol the other crew is training or taking leave

	Date Launched
Vanguard	1992
Victorious	1993
Vengeance	building
Vigilant	building

Fleet Submarines

The Royal Navy operates two classes of Nuclear Powered Attack Submarines (SSN) as follows:

Swiftsure Class	Date Launched
Sovereign	1974
Superb	1976
Sceptre	1978
Spartan	1979
Splendid	1981

Dimensions: Length 82.9m; Beam 9.8m; Draught 8.2m; Displacement 4,200 tons surfaced and 4,500 tons dived; Propulsion - 1 x Rolls Royce pressurised water cooled reactor supplying steam to two sets of General Electric geared turbines delivering 15,000 shp to one shaft; Performance - Max Speed 20 kts surfaced and 30+ kts dived; diving depth 400m (operational) and 600m maximum; Complement 12 officers and 85 ratings; Torpedoes - 5 x 533mm (21″) tubes for 20 x Mk 24 Tigerfish wire guided and Mk 8 anti-ship torpedos; Mines - up to 50 x Mk 5 Stonefish or Mk 6 Sea Urchins instead of torpedoes; Missiles - 5 x UGM-84A Sub Harpoon tube launched anti-ship missiles.

Trafalgar Class	Date Launched
Trafalgar	1983
Turbulent	1984
Tireless	1985

Torbay	1987
Trenchant	1989
Talent	1990
Triumph	1991

Dimensions: Length 85.4m; Beam 9.8m; Draught 8.2m; Displacement 4,700 tons surfaced and 5,200 tons dived; Propulsion - 1 x Rolls Royce pressurised water cooled reactor supplying steam to two sets of General Electric geared turbines delivering 15,000 shp to one shaft; Performance - Max Speed 20 kts surfaced and 32 kts dived; diving depth 400m (operational) and 600m maximum; Complement 12 officers and 85 ratings; Torpedoes - 5 x 533mm (21″) tubes for 20 x Mk 24 Tigerfish wire guided and Mk 8 anti-ship torpedoes; Mines - up to 50 x Mk 5 Stonefish or Mk 6 Sea Urchins instead of torpedoes; Missiles - 5 x UGM-84A Sub Harpoon tube launched anti-ship missiles.

These nuclear-powered fleet submarines are armed with homing torpedoes (range approx 15kms+) that can be used against other submarines or surface vessels. The Sub-Harpoon long-range anti-ship missile (range 110 kms) is now in service as the principal anti-surface ship weapon in these submarines.

Both classes are capable of continuous patrols at high underwater speed, independent of base support, and can circumnavigate the globe without surfacing. Their long endurance and sophisticated weapon systems make them formidable adversaries. There are three decks and although space is restricted, living conditions are comfortable.

In late 1994 the UK MoD stated that "we are exploring the possibility of fitting our SSNs with conventionally armed Tomahawk land-attack missiles procured from the United States. Feasability studies were launched in the autumn, the results of which are expected to be available shortly; a decision on procurement will be taken in the light of the findings of these studies."
The Tomahawk TLAM-C (Tactical Land Attack Missile - Conventional) has a range of about 1,490 kms

Aircraft Carriers

The Royal Navy operates 3 x Aircraft/ASW Carriers of which two are generally available and one is in refit at any one time: These vessels are:

	Commissioned
Invincible	1980
Illustrious	1982
Ark Royal	1985

Major Characteristics - Speed 28 knots; Displacement 16,800 tons (standard) 19,000 (full load); Engines 4 x Rolls Royce Olympus TM3B Gas Turbines delivering 112,000 shp to two shafts; Length 206.6m; Beam 27.5m; Draught 7.3m; Flight Deck Length 167.8m; Complement 131 officers and 870 rates plus an air group of 320.

The primary task of this class of ship is to act as the command ship of anti-submarine warfare forces. They are also effective and flexible command ships for air operations and aircraft from the carriers Invincible and Illustrious were involved in operations in the former Yugoslavia during 1995

All three carriers carry Sea King anti-submarine (ASW) helicopters, Sea King airborne early warning (AEW) helicopters and Sea Harrier aircraft
A typical embarked "air group" could consist of:

> 8 x Sea Harriers
> 8 x Sea King HAS.6 (ASW)
> 3 x Sea King HAS.2 (AEW)

Note: During early September 1995 RAF Chinook helicopters were conducting deck trials on HMS Invincible off the coast of Bosnia.

The Sea Dart medium-range surface-to-air missile is fitted for air defence (with a secondary anti-ship role) and the Phalanx or Goalkeeper rapid- firing gun systems have been fitted to enhance the close-range anti-missile defence capability. A 'ski-jump' launching ramp is fitted to improve the operational take-off performance of the Sea Harrier. The vessels are powered by Rolls-Royce Olympus gas turbine engines and on average these ships took approximately 6-7 years to build.

The UK MoD is known to be looking at replacement vessels due for service around 2010-2015 and three study teams directed by a Studies Steering Group have been commissioned. These three study groups are believed to be looking at three differing platform designs. The first is a a design catering for Conventional Take Off and Landing (CTOL) aircraft, the second would operate aircraft of the Short Take Off and Arrested Recovery (STOBAR) type and the third would operate Advanced Short Take-Off and Vertical Landing (ASTOVL) aircraft.

In the interim HMS Ocean an LPH (Landing Platform Helicopter) is under construction at Govan with a proposed in service date of 1998. The hull of the ship is being built to Merchant Navy standards at a cost of some £170 million. The ship should be able to carry an air group of 12 x Sea King HAS.4 troop lift helicopters and 6 x Lynx HAS.8 attack helicopters (although these could be replaced by EH 101 and Apache by the end of the decade). Current plans are for HMS Ocean to have a crew of 250 and the ship will be capable of carrying a complete Marine Commando (up to 850 personnel).

Assault Ships

Major Characteristics - Speed 21 knots; Displacement 11,582 tons; Engines 2 x sets of English Electric geared steam turbies delivering 22,000 shp to 2 props; Length 158m; Beam 24.3m; Draught 6.2; Complement 50 officers and 50 rates plus air group of 3 officers and 85 rates.

	Commissioned
Fearless	1965
Intrepid	1967

These two vessels are the UK's most versatile vessels for amphibious warfare and proved their worth in the Falklands Campaign. Each is fitted out as a Naval

Assault Group/Brigade HQ from which naval and military personnel, working in close co-operation, can mount and control an amphibious operation.

Both ships can transport a military force complete with full suporting armour.4 x Mk4 Landing craft capable of 35 troops or a 5.5 ton vehicle are carried in davits and the well deck can carry 2 main battle tanks or 100 tons of stores and 4 x LCM (landing craft). Four more main battle tanks can be carried on the tank deck. The ships can also operate a flight of 4 helicopters and are armed with modern close-range guns for air defence. HMS Fearless is fitted with the Phalanx close-in weapon system to enhance the air defence. In an emergency the ships could carry up to 1,000 troops. HMS Intrepid is currently in reserve.

Replacements are planned for both HMS Fearless and HMS Intrepid. In its latest statement (May 1995) the UK MoD said "In last July's (1994) 'Front Line First' statement we confirmed our intention to replace HMS Intrepid and HMS Fearless. An invitation to tender was subsequently issued in August (1994) and we expect to place an order later this year (1995)."

The new ships will probably have two flight deck places for EH 101 helicopters, 4 x LCU landing craft in the well deck and another 4 x landing craft in davits. The crew will probably total some 320 and 300 troops could be carried (possibly 600 in an emergency). If an order is placed in late 1995 it would be unrealistic to expect an in service date before 1999-2000.

Type 42 Destroyers

There are currently 12 x Type 42 Guided Missile Destroyers (DDG) whose primary role is to provide air defence of naval task group operations

	Commissioned	
Birmingham	1976	Batch 1
Cardiff	1979	Batch 1
Newcastle	1978	Batch 1
Glasgow	1979	Batch 1
Exeter	1980	Batch 2
Southampton	1981	Batch 2

Nottingham	1982	Batch 2
Liverpool	1982	Batch 2
Manchester	1982	Batch 3
Gloucester	1985	Batch 3
Edinburgh	1985	Batch 3
York	1985	Batch 3

During 1995 HMS Birmingham and HMS Edinburgh were in refit

Major Characteristics - Speed 29 kts on Olympus turbines or 18kts on Tyne turbines; Range 7,400 kms at 18 kts; Displacement : Batch 1 & 2 - 4,350 full load and Batch 3 - 5,350 at full load; Engines - COGOG Type system with 2 x Rolls Royce Olympus TM3B gas turbines delivering 56,000 shp and 2 x Rolls Royce Tyne RM1A gas turbines delivering 8,500 shp to two shafts; Length 125.6m (Batch 1 & 2) and 141.1m (Batch 3); Beam 14.3m (Batch 1 & 2) and 14.9m (Batch 3); Draught 5.8m; Complement 24 officers and 229 rates (max total 312); Aircraft Carried - Sea Lynx with Sea Skua and/or Stingray torpedoes.

In general these vessels are armed with the Sea Dart medium-range air- defence missile system, which also has an anti-ship capability (1 x Twin Launcher for 24 Sea Dart SAM for Batch 1 & 2 with Batch 3 carrying 40 missiles); the automatic rapid-fire 114mm (4.5-inch) gun with a range of 21 kms, anti-submarine torpedo tubes and the Phalanx rapid-firing gun system for close-range anti-missile defence. They also carry the high speed multi- purpose Lynx helicopter armed with anti-submarine weapons and the Sea Skua anti-ship missile which is controlled by the Sea Spray search radar. The latest communication and sensor equipment is fitted in all Type 42 Destroyers.

All of the Type 42 Destroyers are based at Portsmouth.

Broadsword Class Frigates (Type 22)

From 1 Jan 1996 it would appear that the Royal Navy will be operating 10 x Type 22 Frigates whose primary role is anti-submarine warfare:

Commissioned

Boxer	1983	Batch 2
Beaver	1984	Batch 2
Brave	1986	Batch 2
London	1987	Batch 2
Sheffield	1988	Batch 2
Coventry	1988	Batch 2
Cornwall	1988	Batch 3
Cumberland	1988	Batch 3
Campbeltown	1989	Batch 3
Chatham	1989	Batch 3

During 1995 HMS Cornwall was in refit.

The Batch 1 ships, HMS Broadsword, Battleaxe, Brilliant and Brazen, all commissioned between 1979 and 1982 will be sold to the Brazilian Navy between 1995-97.

Major Characteristics - Speed 30 kts+ on Olympus turbines or 18kts on Tyne turbines; Range 8,370 kms at 18 kts; Displacement 4,600 full load; Engines - COGOG Type system with 2 x Rolls Royce Spey SM1A gas turbines delivering 18,770 shp and 2 x Rolls Royce Tyne RM1A gas turbines delivering 8,500 shp to two shafts; Length 143.6m; Beam 14.8m; Draught 6.0m; Complement 23 officers and 302 rates; Aircraft Carried - 1 or 2 Sea Lynx with Sea Skua and or Stingray torpedoes or 1 x Sea King HAS.6.

Type 22 Figates of both Batch 2 and Batch 3 are capable of not only anti-submarine operations (their primary role) but anti-aircraft and anti-ship roles. Equipped with the latest computer-assisted sonar systems and communications equipment these vessels are highly efficient maritime hunters. Two Lynx anti-submarine helicopters can be carried and anti- submarine torpedo tubes are fitted. Batch 2 vessels carry the Exocet MM38 surface-to-surface missile (range 65 kms) and the Batch 3 vessels the Harpoon surface to surface missile (range 110 kms) Sea Wolf close-range air-defence missile systems provide an all-round defence capability and the 30mm Goalkeeper, defence against incoming missiles. The automatic rapid-fire Vickers Mk 8 DP 114mm (4.5-inch) gun with a range of 21 kms is fitted to the batch 3 ships.

All the ships have controllable-pitch propellers and stabilizers. This class is the first to be designed to the metric system in the Royal Navy.

Duke Class Frigates (Type 23)

Although designed for anti-submarine operations like most new surface combatants of this size this is really a multi-purpose vessel. There are currently 10 ships of this class in service with another three on order.

	Commissioned
Norfolk	1990
Argyll	1991
Marlborough	1991
Lancaster	1991
Iron Duke	1992
Monmouth	1993
Montrose	1993
Westminster	1993
Northumberland	1994
Richmond	1994
Grafton	(1996) (building)
Sutherland	(1996) (building)
Somerset	(1997) (building)

Major Characteristics - Speed 28 kts+; Range 14,400 kms at 15 kts; Displacement 3,500 tons standard; Engines - CODLAG Type system with 2 x Rolls Royce Spey SM1A gas turbines delivering 18,770 shp each; For vessels after HMS Westminster (1994) 2 x Rolls Royce Spey SM1C delivering 26,150 shp each; Length 133m; Beam 16.2m; Draught 5.5m; Complement 12 officers and 157 rates; Aircraft Carried - 1 x Sea Lynx with Sea Skua and/or Stingray torpedoes.

Designed primarily for the anti-submarine (ASW) role, it is fitted with the latest radar and communications systems and towed array sonar. Air defence is provided with a vertical launch Sea Wolf system and the surface armament includes the Harpoon missile system (range 110 kms) and the 114mm (4.5-inch) gun for naval gun fire support. From 1998 the Lynx helicopter will be replaced by the new 'EH 101 Merlin' helicopter when it comes into service. HMS Norfolk, the first of this class, was commissioned in 1990, the latest to be accepted into service being Northumberland and Richmond in 1994. Three more have been ordered and will be named HMS Somerset, HMS Grafton and HMS Sutherland. These ships are powered by a CODLAG system (Combined diesel-electric and gas-turbine propulsion) and the diesel- electric is used for minimum underwater noise during ASW operations. This class will form the backbone of the frigate fleet in the short to medium term.

Common New Generation Frigate (Project HORIZON)

Project HORIZON is a collaborative programme between the UK, France and Italy to procure a new class of Anti-Air Warfare (AAW) frigate. This frigate will replace the UK's existing Type 42 AAW Destroyer and we believe that it would be unrealistic to expect to see this vessel in service before the early part of the next decade.

The Staff Requirement was endorsed in its original form in 1991 as a basis for collaborative negotiations with France following collapse of the NATO AAW frigate project NFR 90. Italy was offered observer status but expressed no active interest until the Autumn of 1992, by which time France and the UK were very close to agreement on a joint Staff Requirement. Italy decided to exercise its option to join with the UK and France to sign a Tripartite Staff Requirement in December 1992.

Collaboration will start with an initial design and validation phase and then proceed to the detailed design and build of three First of Class (FOC) ships. Industry will be encouraged to identify savings arising from common support. Development of the whole ship, including construction of the three FOC ships and the physical integration of the combat system will be contracted to a French - Italian - UK joint venture company. A consortium led by GEC (with BAe and others) was selected in January 1994 as the UK member of the joint venture company.

A Joint Project Office has been established in London with full centralised authority for technical, financial and contractual functions. As host nation, the UK provides the necessary contractual and financial infrastructure. Plans for signature of a Tripartite Programme MOU have been delayed due to continuing differences with France and Italy over the Principal Anti-Air Missile System (PAAMS) for the ship.

Combat Management Systems (CMS) project definition (PD) for the project will probably start in January 1996 - about 18 months later than expected.
Original plans were for the UK to procure 12 vessels at the rate of 2 per year starting in 2002.

Hunt Class - Mine Counter Measures Vessels (MCMV)

	Commissioned		Commissioned
Brecon	1979	Chiddingford	1984
Ledbury	1981	Hurworth	1985
Cattistock	1982	Bicester	1986
Cottesmore	1983	Atherstone	1987

Brocklesby	1982	Berkley	1987
Middleton	1984	Quorn	1989
Dulverton	1983		

Major Characteristics - Speed 17 kts+; Displacement 625 tons standard; Engines 2 x Rushton Paxman Deltic 9-59K Diesels; Length 57m; Beam 10m; Draught 2.2m; Complement 6 officers and 39 rates:

The first of this advanced class of GRP-built mine countermeasures vessels, HMS Brecon, entered service in 1979, 13 are now in service, and are due a mid-life update starting in 2000. They are equipped with Remote Control Mine Disposal System (RCMDS1) and are fitted with Influence Sweeps and a 30mm gun.

Single Role Minehunter

	Commissioned		Commissioned
Sandown	1989	Grimsby	Building
Inverness	1991	Bangor	Building
Cromer	1991	Ramsey	Building
Walney	1993	Blyth	Building
Bridport	1993	Shoreham	Building
Penzance	Building	Pembroke	Building

Major Characteristics - Speed 15 kts+; Displacement 378 tons lights; Engines 2 x Paxman Valentia 6RPA 200-EM 1500 Diesels; Range 2,600 kms at 11 Kts; Length 52.7m; Beam 10.5m; Draught 2.30m; Complement 5 officers and 29 rates.

HMS Sandown, the first of the new Single-Role Minehunter class entered service in 1989, and HMS Bridport, the latest, entered service in 1993. They are built of GRP and complement the Hunt Class MCMVs. Sandown Class vessels are equipped with a minehunting sonar and mine disposal equipment making them capable of dealing with mines at depths of up to 200m. Each ship carries 2 x Mk2 Remote Control Mine Disposal Systems (Submersibles) capable of identifying and disposing of mines up to 300m. 1 x 30mm Oerlikon gun is carried for local defence. Seven more of this class have been ordered.

Fishery Protection and Offshore Patrol Vessels

Fishery protection and patrolling Britain's offshore gas and oilfield installations is carried out by the Royal Navy's Fishery Protection Squadron.

Island Class

	Commissioned
Alderney	1979
Guernsey	1977
Anglesey	1979
Lindisfarne	1978
Orkney	1977
Shetland	1977

Major Characteristics - Speed 16.5 kts+; Displacement 998 tons standard; Engines 2 x Rushton 12 RK 3CM Diesels; Range 11,000 kms at 12 Kts; Length 61m; Beam 11m; Draught 4.27m; Complement 5 officers and 29 rates.

Six Island Class patrol vessels form the Offshore Division which, in addition to their fishery protection tasks outside the 12-mile coastal limit, carry out regular surveillance patrols of the offshore gas and oilfield installations.
The vessels are armed with 1 x 40mm Bofors AA Gun.

Castle Class

	Commissioned
Leeds Castle	1981
Dumbarton Castle	1982

Major Characteristics - Speed 20kts; Displacement 1,350 tons standard; Engines 2 x Rushton 12 RK 320DM Diesels; Range 10,000 kms at 12 Kts; Length 81m; Beam 11.5m; Draught 3.42m; Complement 6 officers and 39 rates plus 25 Royal Marines as required.

The two Castle Class patrol vessels which are in service with the Offshore Division have a landing deck and fuelling facilities for the Sea King helicopter. Armament consists of 1 x 30mm Oerlikon and 2 x 7.62mm MG.
One of these vessels is generally on patrol around the area of the Falklands Islands.

River Class Minesweepers

Major Characteristics - Speed 14 kts+; Displacement 630 tons standard; Engines 2 x Rushton 6 RKCM Diesels; Range 4,500 at 10 kts; Length 47.6m; Beam 10.5m; Draught 3.10m; Complement 7 officers and 23 rates; Armament 1 x 40mm Bofors AA - 2 x 7.62mm MG.

The Northern Ireland Squadron consists of River Class minesweepers. HMS Blackwater, Arun, Itchen and Spey. The primary task of these vessels is to deter the movement of arms, munitions and personnel of the various terrorist factions that exist within the province. These four vessels were commissioned in 1984/85 and are the survivors of a class that originally totalled 12. One more River Class Minesweeper, HMS Orwell is the training vessel of BRNC Dartmouth

Peacock Class

Major Characteristics - Speed 28 kts+; Displacement 664 tons standard; Engines 2 x APE Crossley SEMT-Pielstick 19PA6V280 Diesels; Range 2,500 at 17 kts; Length 62m; Beam 10m; Draught 2.72m; Complement 6 officers and 25 rates; Armament 1 x 76mm Oto Melara Compact DP; 4 x 7.62mm MG

The patrol craft HMS Peacock, Plover and Starling are based at Hong Kong for policing duties around the island. They are armed with a 76mm gun and close-range weapons. They also carry Fast Pursuit Craft (FPC) to enable interception and boarding parties to function effectively. The three vessels were commissioned in 1983/84.

Survey Ships
Commissioned

Hecla	1965	Ocean Survey
Herald	1974	Ocean Survey

Major Characteristics - Speed 14 kts+; Displacement 2,510 tons standard; Engines 3 x Paxman Ventura 12YJCZ Diesels; Range 12,000 at 11 kts; Length 79.3m; Beam 14.9m; Draught 4.0m; Complement 12 officers and 116 rates.

Note: Charateristics relate to HMS Herald which is an improved Hecla Class vessel

	Commissioned	
Beagle	1968	Coastal Survey Vessels
Bulldog	1968	Coastal Survey Vessels

Major Characteristics - Speed 15 kts ; Displacement 800 tons standard; Engines 4 x Lister Blackstone ERS-8-M Diesels; Range 4,600 at 12 kts; Length 60.9m; Beam 11.43; Draught 3.6m; Complement 5 officers and 34 rates

Roebuck	1986	Coastal Survey Vessel

Major Characteristics - Speed 15 kts ; Displacement 1,059 tons standard; Engines 4 x Mirrless ES-8 Mk 1 Diesels; Range 4,000 at 10 kts; Length 63.8m; Beam 13m; Draught 3.65m; Complement 8 officers and 34 rates.

	Commissioned	
Gleaner	1983	Surveying Motor Vessel

Major Characteristics - Speed 14 kts; Displacement 20tons standard; Length 14.8m; Complement 1 officer and 4 rates.

The Royal Navy's Surveying Service has been operating throughout the world since the formation of the Hydrographic Department in 1795 and the information from oceanographic surveys is used for producing Admiralty charts and nautical publications which have a world-wide sale and are used by ships of many nations

The Surveying Flotilla consists of ocean-going ships, coastal vessels and inshore craft. In addition to surveying in overseas areas, many of the flotilla are constantly engaged in updating the charts covering the waters around the United Kingdom.

To carry out these wide-ranging tasks the latest surveying techniques are employed, including digitised echo sounders, side scan sonar, automated plotting and recording of position, depth, gravity and magnetic parameters
Satellite and inertial navigation systems are used when out of range of shore-based position fixing systems.

Ice Patrol Ship

Major Characteristics - Speed 12 kts ; Displacement 6,500 tons standard; Engines 2 x Ulstein Bergen BRM-8 Diesels; Range 5,000 kms at 12 kts; Length 91m; Beam 17.9m; Draught 6.5m; Complement 15 officers and 97 rates and 15 Royal Marines.

In srvice with the Royal Navy since 1990 HMS Endurance (previously MV Polar Circle) supports British interests in the South Atlantic and Antarctic waters, working alongside members of the British Antarctic Survey Team, carrying out hydrographic surveying, meteorological work and research programmes. It has a flight deck and hangar for Lynx helicopters. The hull is painted red for easy recognition in the ice.

HMS Invincible launching Sea Harriers (Crown Copyright).

HMS Brave and HMS Sheffield refuelling at sea from RFA Bayleaf (Crown Copyright).

Hunt Class MCMV HMS Middleton at Sea (Crown Copyright).

Royal Marines with SA 80 rifles (Crown Copyright).

Royal Yacht - HMY Britannia

Major Characteristics - Speed 21 kts ; Displacement 3,900 tons standard; Engines 2 x sets of geared steam turbines; Range 3,675 kms at 14 kts; Length 125.9m; Beam 16.76m; Draught 4.8m; Complement 21 officers and 256 rates.

Commissioned in 1953 HMS Britannia was designed as a medium-sized naval hospital ship for 200 patients, in addition to being used by Her Majesty The Queen in peacetime.

The vessel's construction conforms to normal mercantile standards and the ship is also fitted with Denny-Brown single fin stabilizers to reduce roll in bad weather. The ship has a modern clipper bow and a modified cruiser stern instead of the traditional swan-bow and counter stern of previous royal yachts.

HMY Britannia is almost certainly going to be phased out of service at the end of the decade and there do not appear to be any official plans for a replacement vessel. During early 1995 there were indications that British Industry was considering providing a replacement.

Training Ships

Major Characteristics - Speed 22.5 kts ; Displacement 44 tons standard; Engines Perkins CVM 800T Diesels; Range 500kms at 15 kts; Length 20.8m; Beam 5.8m; Draught 1.8m; Complement 11-15 total; Armament 1 x 20mm AA Gun and 2 x 7.62mm MG (Ranger and Trumpeter only).

	Commissioned		Commissioned
Archer	1985	Puncher	1988
Biter	1985	Charger	1988
Smiter	1985	Ranger	1988

Pursuer	1985	Trumpeter	1988
Blazer	1988	Example	1985
Dasher	1988	Explorer	1985
Exploit	1988	Express	1988

Fourteen Fast Training Boats are in service with the Inshore Training Squadron (ITS) based a Rosyth. The Archer and Example Class supported by the Fleet Tenders Loyal Watcher and Loyal Chancellor are mainly used as University Training Ships. HMS Ranger and Trumpeter are used as Gibraltar Search and Rescue Craft.

Royal Fleet Auxiliary Service

The Royal Navy describes the The Royal Fleet Auxiliary Service as "The specialist front-line support force for the Royal Navy that replenishes warships at sea with fuel, stores and weapons. The service is unique in that all the Royal Navy's major Auxiliaries are civilian manned. The RFA service is part of the Royal Naval Supply and Transport Service and employs some 2,500 officers and ratings who follow the traditional paths of the Merchant Navy to obtain their basic qualifications, but with a substantial overlay of naval training to develop the skills needed in an operational environment. The 21 ships of the Fleet include both large and small Fleet Tankers, Support Tankers, Landing Ships Logistic, an Aviation Training Ship and a Forward Repair ship. Since it was formed in 1905, the RFA service has pioneered and perfected the art of Replenishment at Sea (RAS). RFA vessels ae now fitted wth close range small calibre self defence weapons and decoys which are manned and maintained by RFA personnel."

Fleet Tankers

	In-Service
Olwen	1965
Olna	1966
Grey Rover	1970
Gold Rover	1974
Black Rover	1974

RFAs Olwen and Olna are purpose-built fast Fleet Tankers capable of supporting Naval task groups in the front line with fuel, lubricants and a limited range of stores. The ability of each of these vessels is further enhanced by the provisions of facilities to embark and operate the Royal Navy's ASW Sea King and Lynx helicopters. Both ships are capable of speeds of up to 20 kts carrying 18,000 tons of fuel oil, 1,720 tons of diesel, 3,730 tons of aircraft fuel and 130 tons of lube oil.

There are also three small fleet tankers of the Rover class. These relatively fast and highly manoeuvrable vessels are able to replenish warships with fuel and a limited amount of dry cargo and refrigerated stores. Although they do not normally carry their own helicopter, they are fitted with a flight deck, but no hangar, and are capable of providing a forward operating base for deploying helicopters if they require fuel.

Rover Class tankers can carry 7,460 cubic metres of fuel; 26 cubic metres of water; 70 cubic metres of lube oil and 600 cubic metres of aviation fuel or gasoline at a sustained speed of 17 kts.

Support Tankers

	In Service
Brambleleaf	1980
Orangeleaf	1982
Bayleaf	1982
Oakleaf	1981

In general the Royal Navy's Support Tankers have the duel role of replenishing warships and fleet tankers at sea and the bulk movement of fuels between naval supply depots. Expect RFA Oakleaf to be able to carry 43,020 cubic metres of fuel in 16 tanks and and the remaining three (Appleleaf Class) tankers approximately 35,000 cubic metres of fuel in 24 tanks. RFA Oakleaf has a crew of 36 and the other three vessels about 65 in total.

Fleet Replenishment Ships

	In Service		In Service
Resource	1967	Fort Victoria	1992
Fort Grange	1978	Fort George	1993
Fort Austin	1979		

RFA Resource is an ammunition, food and stores ship currently believed to be operating at Spit in Croatia in support of United Nations Forces. The ship has seven holds and displaces 22,800 tons. There is a crew of 134 Royal Fleet Auxiliary and 37 civilian staff.

Fort Victoria and Fort George are also ammunition, food and stores ships both capable of operating up to five Sea King helicopters with full maintenance facilities onboard. Displacing 22,749 tons and capable of carrying about 12,000 cubic metres in four holds, including 2,300 cubic metres of refrigerated stores, both of these ships have a crew of 127 RFA, 36 civilian staff and 45 Royal Naval personnel.

Aviation Training Ship

RFA Argus was launched in 1981 and was formerly the container ship MV Contender Bezant. In 1982 the vessel was used as an aircraft transport during the Falklands War and was purchased by the Royal Navy during 1984.

The ship operates Lynx and Sea King helicopters and transports Sea Harriers. RFA Argus is managed and operated by the RFA Service but there is a sizeable Royal Naval Aviation Group embarked. In 1991 during the Gulf War RFA Argus was used as a Primary Casualty Receiving Ship. The complement is generally about 75 x RFA personnel, 28 x RN personnel and a training group of some 130 RN personnel. In an emergency the ship could probably carry up to 700 troops.

Forward Repair Ship

Launched in 1981 and named the Stena Inspector the ship was originally chartered during the Falklands War and taken into Royal Naval Service as RFA Diligence during 1984. RFA Diligence is a general repair and maintenance ship and capable of providing specialised maintenance support across the fleet. The vessel is particularly useful when Task Forces are operating far from home bases and in the past has provided particularly valuable support especially in the Gulf during 1991.

Landing Ships Logistic

	In Service
Sir Geraint	1967
Sir Bedivere	1966
Sir Percivale	1967
Sir Tristram	1966 (rebuilt 1985)
Sir Galahad	1988

The five LSLs in service with the RFA are each capable of carrying approximately 400 troops and there is a beaching cargo capacity of 3,440 tons. Heavy stores and equipment are carried including armoured vehicles and the ships are fitted with bow and stern loading doors and ramps. They are capable of beach landings and the operation of helicopters. During the Falklands Campaign two LSLs sustained heavy damage. RFA Sir Tristram was subsequently redesigned, rebuilt and re-entered service in late 1985. RFA Sir Galahad was later sunk and designated an official War Grave with a new RFA Sir Galahad entering service in 1988. Sir Bedivere is currently (mid 1995) undergoing a Ship Life Extension Programme.

Royal Maritime Auxiliary Service (RMAS)

The Royal Maritime Auxiliary Service (RMAS) provides the Royal Navy with the wide variety of waterborne services needed at naval bases. Marine Services has taken its present shape during the past 30 years by combining the areas formerly managed by Captains of Dockyards, Senior Victualling, Armament Supply, and Naval Stores Officers. This was followed by the amalgamation in 1975 of the separate Marine Services suh as Ocean Tugs, Admiralty Cable Ships, trials vessels, and the Mooring and Salvage service into the present organisation

The RMAS operates about 400 vessels and lighters and is a unified service manned by a civilian staff of some 425 officers and 1,250 junior staff.

Tasks include the provision of tugs and pilots for harbour movements, ocean and coastal towing; moorings, salvage and diving operations, the transport of personnel, fuel, water, stores and ammunition; torpedo recovery, degaussing, Fleet trials support, tank cleaning, sullage, pollution control, and marine range safety duties.

RMAS vessels are allocated to the UK Naval bases at Portsmouth, Devonport, Rosyth, Portland, the Clyde, Pembroke Dock, Kyle of Lochalsh and Gibraltar. RMAS vessels are easily recognised by their buff-coloured funnels and superstructure and their black hulls, which have an all-round white riband at deck level. They fly the blue ensign, which is defaced in the fly by a yellow anchor above two yellow wavy lines.

Support operations are carried out mainly in UK waters with occasional overseas deployments ranging from the Mediterranean to the Falklands.

Fleet Air Arm

The Fleet Air Arm provides the air support for the Royal Navy and the Royal Marines. Harrier Squadrons are embarked on the three carriers HMS Ark Royal, HMS Illustrious and HMS Invincible, as are detachments of the airborne early warning and anti submarine Sea King helicopter squadrons.

The majority of RN ships of the destroyer/frigate type have their own anti submarine/anti ship Lynx aircraft that also serve a vital fleet communications role. Whilst not strictly part of the Fleet Air Arm, the Royal Marines 3 Cdo Bde Air Sqn is a Royal Naval organisation that provides communications and anti tank helicopter support for Commando forces operating ashore. The overall current Fleet Air Arm basic structure is as follows:

Air Defence/Recce/Attack

800 Sqn	801 Sqn	899 Sqn
Yeovilton	Yeovilton	Yeovilton
6 x Sea Harrier	6 x Sea Harrier	6 x Sea Harrier FRS1, F/A2
FRS1, F/A2	FRS1, F/A2	4 x Harrier T4

Anti Submarine

810 Sqn	814 Sqn	819 Sqn	820 Sqn	706 Sqn
Culdrose	Culdrose	Prestwick	Culdrose	Culdrose
13 x Sea King	7 x Sea King	9 x Sea King	7 x Sea King	11 x Sea King
HAS 5/6	HAS 5/6	HAS 5/6	HAS 5/6	HAS 5/6

(1) Aircraft in these squadrons are often deployed in flights of single or multiple aircraft

Anti Submarine/Anti Ship

815 Sqn (2)	702 Sqn
Portland	Portland
Approx 38 x Lynx	12 x Lynx
HAS 2/3,	HMA 8HAS 2/3,
HMA 8	

(2) The majority of 815 Squadron's aircraft are at sea on board RN Frigates/Destroyers. Of the squadron total - about 25-30 aircraft are probably assigned to ships at any one time.

Commando Air Assault

845 Sqn	846 Sqn	707 Sqn
Yeovilton	Yeovilton	Yeovilton
8 x Sea King	8 x Sea King	8 x Sea King
HC4	HC4	HC4

Aircrew Training

```
        ┌────────────────────────┐
705 Sqn                          750 Sqn
Culdrose                         Culdrose
17 x Gazelle HT2                 13 x Jetstream T2/3
```

In addition to the above the Fleet Air Arm has the following:

Airborne Early Warning	849 Sqn	Culdrose	8 x Sea King AEW2
Fleet Support & SAR	771 Sqn	Culdrose	5 x Sea King Mk5
	772 Sqn	Portland	6 x Sea King Mk4
3 Cdo Bde Air Sqn		Yeovilton	7 x Gazelle/ 6 x Lynx Mk7

Sea Harrier

In Service With:

800 Sqn	6 x Sea Harrier FRS1, F/A2GR7	RNAS Yeovilton
801 Sqn	6 x Sea Harrier FRS1, F/A2GR7	RNAS Yeovilton
899 Sqn	6 x Sea Harrier FRS1, F/A2GR7	RNAS Yeovilton
	4 x Sea Harrier T4	RNAS Yeovilton

F/A2 (FRS2) Crew 1; Length Overall 14.17m; Wingspan 7.70m; Height 3.71m; Max Level Speed 1185 km/ph (736mph) at low level; Max Take Off Weight approx 11,880 kgs (26,200lbs); Armament - Able to carry bombs, rockets, guns, missiles and flares attached to 4 x wing weapon pylons and 1 x underfuselage weapon pylon; Engine 1 x Rolls-Royce Pegasus Mk 2 vectored thrust turbofan; Ferry Attack Radius 463 kms (288 miles).

In service with the Royal Navy since 1979, the Sea Harrier has been improved and updated to cope with the technological changes that the changing threat has posed. The aircraft remains the most advanced ship-borne short take off and vertical landing (STOVL) aircraft in the world.

The aircraft has a maritime figher/reconnaissance/strike role and proved itself as an effective, flexible and reliable aircraft in the Falklands Campaign, where 29 aircraft flew over 2,300 sorties and destroyed 22 enemy aircraft in air-to-air combat without loss. The original version in Royal Naval Service was the FRS1 with the newer F/A2 (FRS2) variant entering service in 1994. The FRS2 differs from the earlier model in that it has a Blue Vixen look-down/shoot down radar combined with the fire and forget Advanced Medium Range Air-to-Air Missile (AMRAAM) which allows the aircraft to engage targets beyond visual range. In addition the Sea Eagle (anti-ship missile) and laser guided bombs can be carried.
The STOVL capability of the Sea Harrier enables the aircraft to operate from the flight deck of an aircraft carrier without the use of catapult- assisted take-off and arrester-wire equipment. "Ski-jump" launching ramps that improve the aircraft's take off performance are fitted to all three of the Royal Navy's aircraft carriers.

F/A2 aircraft are now entering service and there are 18 on order from British Aerospace. The remaining FRS1 aircraft are recieving their mid-life update to bring them up to the A/A2 standard. The T4 is a two seat trainer version of the Harrier.

Expect a Sea Harrier Squadron to have 9 established crews

Sea King

In Service With:

810 Sqn	Sea King HAS 5/6	13
814 Sqn	Sea King HAS 5/6	7
819 Sqn	Sea King HAS 5/6	9
820 Sqn	Sea King HAS 5/6	7
706 Sqn	Sea King HAS 5/6	11

849 Sqn	Sea King AEW 2	9
845 Sqn	Sea King HC4	8
846 Sqn	Sea King HC4	8
848 Sqn	Sea King HC4	8
771 Sqn	Sea King Mk5	5
772 Sqn	Sea King Mk4	5

HAS Mk 5/6: Crew 2 on flight deck and 2 in cabin; Fuselage Length 17.01m; Width 3.78m; Height 4.72m; Weight (empty) 6201 kg; Max Take Off Weight 9525 kg; Rotor Diameter 18.9m; Cruising Speed 208 km/ph (129mph) at sea level; Service Ceiling 1,220m; Mission Radius(with 2 hours on station and carrying 3 x torpedoes) 231 kms (144 miles); Engines 2 x Rolls Royce Gnome H.1400 IT turboshafts mounted side by side above the cabin; Armament such as 7.62mm MG or 40mm Grenade Launchers can be fitted where appropriate

The Westland Sea King is a license built version of the US Sikorsky S-61 and the Royal Navy's HAS Mark 1 aircraft's first flight was in 1969. Since that time the aircraft has been extensively upgraded and passed through a series of Marks.

The current situation is that the Royal Navy operates the HAS Mk 5/6 in the anti submarine role. The aircraft can remain on station for long periods up to 100 miles from the ship and can search for submarine targets using either its own sonar bouys or those dropped by maritime patrol aircraft such as Nimrods. Targets that have been located are then attacked with torpedoes or depth charges The AEW 2 is used for airborne early warning and is a Sea King HAS Mark 2 fitted with a Thorn EMI Search Water radar carried in a radardome that can be swivelled down underneath the aircraft for operational searches. A detachment of three AEW 2 aircraft generally deploys with each aircraft carrier.

The Sea King HC4 (Commando) is a tactical military helicopter capable of transporting 28 fully equipped troops or 6,000 lbs (2,720 kgs) as an internal load. Carrying 28 troops the aircraft has a range of about 246 miles (396 kms). The first HC4 deliveries were made to the Royal Navy in 1979.

The Mk 5 aircraft in service with 771 Sqn are SAR aircraft (Search & Rescue). RN SAR aircraft are stationed at Prestwick, Culdrose and Portland.

Lynx

In Service With:

815 Sqn	Lynx HAS 3, HMA 8	38
702 Sqn	Lynx HAS 3, HMA 8	12
3 Cdo Bde Air Sqn	Lynx Mk 7	6

Crew - 2 On the flightdeck and up to 2 mission crew in the fuselage; Length Fuselage 11.92m: Height 3.2m: Rotor Diameter 12.8m: Max Speed 144mph (232kph) at sea level: Ferry Range 1046 kms (650 miles) with max internal and external fuel tanks; Engines 2 Rolls-Royce Gem Mk 42 Turboshafts; Weight (max take off) 4,876kg (10,750lbs).

Lynx aircraft are at sea with all frigates and destroyers to provide anti- surface surveillance and anti-submarine warfare (ASW) capabilities. With the introduction into service of the first of the upgraded 44 x HAS 3, HMA 8 aircraft in late 1994/early 1994 the Lynx in Royal Naval service has been turned from an anti-submarine helicopter into a dedicated maritime attack aircraft. Capable of carrying anti-submarine torpedoes (range 10kms) and anti-ship Sea Skua missiles (range 20kms) the HMA 8 is capable of integrating its navigational, communications and fighting systems through a 1553B databus.

Typical combat mission profiles in the anti-submarine role could be a patrol out to 60 miles, a two hour loiter in the search area carrying torpedoes and smoke markers etc and return.

EH 101 Merlin

The Royal Navy has 44 x EH 101 Merlin ASW helicopters on order in a contract worth £1.5 billion. The "in service date" is 1998 and by the early part of the next decade the Merlin should have replaced the ASW Sea Kings and some of the ASW Lynx in Royal Naval service. The cost of the contract was worth 1.5 billion. Trials aircraft are flying and extensive sea trials were held on HMS Iron Duke in 1993. The first production aircraft is due off the production line in 1996

Royal Naval Missiles

Exocet MM38

Length 5.21m; Diameter 0.45m; Total Weight 750 kgs; Range 45 kms.

Exocet MM38 is a medium range surface launched anti- ship missile and is carried in the Type 22 Batch 2 frigates. The guidance system is active radar terminal homing.

Sea Wolf

Length 1.91m; Diameter 0.18m; Total Weight 79.8 kgs; Range 6/7000m; Altitude 3/4000m.

Sea Wolf is a ship based, surface to air missile designed for the defence of point targets. This is a highly efficient system thought to be capable of dealing with aircraft, missiles and even artillery rounds. The guidance system is semi-automatic command to line-of-sight with radar and/or infra- red missile and target tracking.

Sea Skua

Length 2.85m; Diameter 0.22m; Total Weight 147 kgs; Range 20kms approx.

Sea Skua is a short range, anti-ship missile that has been in Royal Naval service since 1982. The missile is currently carried as the main armament of the Lynx aircraft flying from RN destroyers/frigates. The guidance system is semi-active terminal homing.

Sea Dart

Length 4.40m; Diameter 0.42m; Total Weight 549 kgs; Range 80kms+ approx.

Sea Dart is a surface to air missile system with a long range (probably in excess of 80kms) and employs a two stage system with a primary booster rocket powering the warhead and ramjet on their way to the target. There is a limited surface to surface capability out to a range of about 28kms and the guidance system is a semi-active homing radar.

Harpoon

Length 3.84m: Diameter 0.343m: Total Weight 526kg: Warhead Weight 225kg: Range 110kms.

Harpoon, manufactured by McDonnel Douglas of the USA, is an extremely powerful anti-shipping missile that is fitted to the Type 22 and Type 23 Frigates. The Sub-Harpoon (UGM-84A) is fitted to the Trafalgar and Swiftsure Class submarines. The latest versions of this missile have extremely sophisticated electronic counter measures (ECM), and the ability to fly a sea skimming course on a dog-leg path through three pre-programmed way points. The warhead is extremely powerful and a hit from Harpoon is almost certain to result in the destruction or disablement of a major surface vessel.

Other Missiles

Missiles in Royal Naval Service such as: AMRAAM, Sea Eagle and Sidewinder are also in RAF service and the relevant entries are in the RAF Section (Part 4).

The Royal Marines

Although the Royal Marines (RM) are an organisation that is part of the Royal Navy, they are trained and equipped for warfare or operations on land, and because of their current role it is very likely that they could be involved in operations and exercises with allied marine and army units.

The Royal Marines number approximately 7,500 officers and men and their primary task is the reinforcement of Norway and NATO's Northern Flank, should a threat develop in that area.

The Royal Marines also have detachments on 12 ships at sea and a number of smaller units world-wide with widely differing tasks. However, the bulk of the manpower of the Royal Marines is grouped in battalion sized organisations known as Commandos (Cdo). There are 3 Commando Groups and they are part of a larger formation known as 3 Commando Brigade (3 Cdo Bde).

Special Boat Service (SBS)

This organisation is the Naval equivalent of the Army's SAS (Special Air Service). Personnel are all volunteers from the mainstream Royal Marines and vacancies are few with competition for entry fierce. Generally speaking only about 30% of volunteers manage to complete the entry course and qualify. The SBS specialise in mounting clandestine operations against targets at sea, in rivers or harbours and against occupied coastlines.

Comacchio Company

This specialist company was formed in 1980, and has the task of guarding the UK's oil rigs and other associated installations from a variey of threats - in particular terrorist attacks.

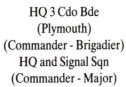

HQ 3 Cdo Bde
(Plymouth)
(Commander - Brigadier)
HQ and Signal Sqn
(Commander - Major)

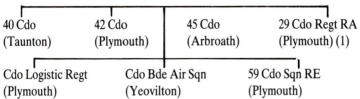

40 Cdo	42 Cdo	45 Cdo	29 Cdo Regt RA
(Taunton)	(Plymouth)	(Arbroath)	(Plymouth) (1)

Cdo Logistic Regt	Cdo Bde Air Sqn	59 Cdo Sqn RE
(Plymouth)	(Yeovilton)	(Plymouth)

Note: (1) 29 Cdo Regt RA has one battery stationed at Arbroath with 45 Cdo

Commando Organisation
Cdo HQ
(Commander - Lt Colonel RM)

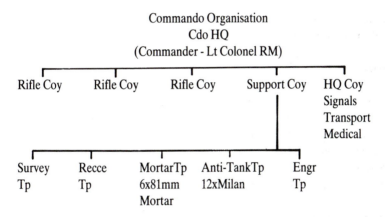

Rifle Coy	Rifle Coy	Rifle Coy	Support Coy	HQ Coy
				Signals
				Transport
				Medical

Survey	Recce	MortarTp	Anti-TankTp	Engr
Tp	Tp	6x81mm	12xMilan	Tp
		Mortar		

Note: A troop (Tp) equates to an army platoon. Each rifle company has three troops. A Royal Marine rifle company is generally commanded by a Captain RM

Royal Marine Listing

Headquarters Royal Marines	-	Portsmouth
HQ 3 Commando Brigade	-	Plymouth (Stonehouse)
3 Commando Bde HQ & Signal Sqn	-	Plymouth (Stonehouse 3
Commando Bde Air Sqn	-	RNAS Yeovilton

73

40 Commando	-	**Taunton**
42 Commando	-	Plymouth (Bickleigh)
45 Commando	-	Arbroath (Condor)
Commando Logistic Regiment	-	Plymouth (Marsh Mills)
539 Assault Sqn	-	Plymouth (Turnchapel)
Comacchio Group	-	Arbroath (Condor)
Commando Training Centre	-	Lympstone
Royal Marines Stonehouse	-	Plymouth
Royal Marines Poole	-	Poole
Amphibious Training & Trials Unit	-	Bideford

There are Royal Marine Reserve Units in London, Bristol, Birkenhead, Glasgow and Newcastle Upon Tyne.

PART 3 - THE BRITISH ARMY

British Army Major Units

(at 1 Jan 1996)	Germany	UK	Elsewhere	TA
Armoured Regts	6	3	-	-
Armoured Recce Regts	1	1	-	5
Armd Infantry Bns	6	2	-	-
Mechanised Bns	-	4	-	-
Airmobile Bns	-	2	-	-
Parachute Bns	-	3	-	2
Light Role Bns	-	19	2	34
Gurkha Battalions	-	1	2	-
SAS Regiments	-	1	-	2
Army Air Corps Regiments	1	4	-	1
Artillery Field Regts	4	8	-	2
Air Defence Regts	1	3	-	3
HAC	-	-	-	1
Engineer Regiments	4	6	-	9
Signals Regiments	3	6	2	11
EW Regiment	1	-	-	-
Equipment Support Bns	3	2	-	4
Logistic Regiments	9	15	2	11
Fd Ambulances/Hospitals	4	10	-	23

Notes: The total manpower strength of the British Army at 1 April 1995 was:

Officers	14,000	(900)
Other Ranks	97,800	(6,300)
	117,800	**(7,200)**

Figures in brackets relate to personel undergoing basic training.

British Army Equipment Summary

Armour: 390 x Challenger 1 - 386 Challenger 2 on order (probably 50 in service on 1 Jan 1996); 140 x Sabre (approx); 88 x Striker; 290 x Scimitar; 2,000 x Fv

432; 789 x MCV 80 Warrior; 400 x Spartan; 644 x Saxon. Awaiting Disposal - Approx 850 x Chieftain; 271 x Scorpion.

Artillery: 500 x 81mm Mortar; 2093 x 51mm Light Mortar; 50 x M109A1; 179 x AS 90 on order; 64 x 227mm MLRS (deliveries continue); 72 x FH 70; 212 x 105mm Light Gun.

Air Defence: 120 x Rapier Fire Units; 40 x Tracked Rapier; 382 x Javelin Launchers; 135 x Starstreak HVM deliveries commencing.
Army Aviation: 126 x Lynx ; 30 x Scout; 159 Gazelle; 7 x BN-2; 7 x DHC2 and 21 Chipmunk (for training).; 67 x Apache on Order; Helicopters available from RAF - 31 x Chinook; 54 x Wessex; 37 x Puma.

The Army Board

The routine management of the Army is the responsibility of The Army Board the composition of which is as follows:

The Secretary of State for Defence
Minister of State (Armed Forces)
Minister of State (Defence Procurement)
Parliamentary Under-Secretary of State for the Armed Forces
Chief of the General Staff
Second Permanent Under Secretary of State
Adjutant General
Quartermaster General
Master General of the Ordnance
Commander in Chief (Land Command)
Commander UK Support Command (Germany)
Assistant Chief of the General Staff

Decisions made by The Defence Council or the Army Board are acted upon by the military staff at the various headquarters world-wide. The Chief of the General Staff is the officer responsible for the Army's contribution to the national defence effort and he maintains control through the commander and the staff branches of each of these headquarters.

Chief of The General Staff (1 Jan 1996)

General Sir Charles Guthrie GCB LVO OBE ADC Gen
Chief of The General Staff

General Sir Charles Guthrie was born on 17 November 1938. He went to The Royal Military Academy Sandhurst in 1957 and was commissioned into the Welsh Guards in 1959. He served with his Regiment as a young officer in the United Kingdom, Germany and Aden. In 1966 he became a Troop Commander with 22nd Special Air Service Regiment and served in Aden, the Persian Gulf, Malaysia and East Africa. In 1968 as a Squadron Commander, still serving with 22nd Special Air Service Regiment he served in the Persian Gulf and the United Kingdom.

He returned to 1st Battalion Welsh Guards in Munster in 1970 to command a mechanised infantry company prior to attending the Staff College at Camberley in 1972. His first appointment after attending the Staff College was Military Assistant to the Chief of the General Staff (Field Marshal Lord Carver and General Sir Peter Hunt). After a year as Second in Command of 1st Battalion Welsh Guards in Cyprus in 1976 he assumed the appointment of Brigade Major, Household Division. In 1977 he commanded 1st Battalion Welsh Guards in Berlin and Northern Ireland.

He became Colonel General Staff, Ministry of Defence in 1980 (Col GS MO2) responsible for military operations and planning worldwide, less Germany and Northern Ireland. In the same year he was Commander British Forces New Hebrides (Vanuatu). In 1981 he was appointed Commander of the 4th Armoured Brigade in Munster, following which he was Chief of Staff, Headquarters 1st (British) Corps in Bielefeld.

He was appointed General Officer Commanding the 2nd Infantry Division and North East District in 1985. He was appointed Colonel Commandant of the Intelligence Corps in 1986. He became Assistant Chief of the General Staff in November 1987 and assumed command of the 1st (British) Corps in October 1989. In January 1992 he became Commander Northern Army Group and Commander-in-Chief British Army of the Rhine. Northern Army Group was disbanded in June 1993. He was appointed ADC Gen on 13 July 1993 and GCB in The Queen's Birthday Honours List in 1994. On 15 March 1994 he was appointed Chief of the General Staff (CGS).

Chain of Command.

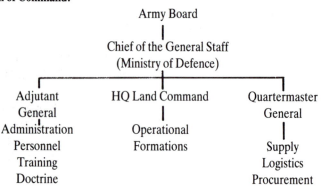

The Army is controlled from the MOD via the above three subsidiary headquarters and a number of smaller headquarters world-wide. The diagram illustrates this chain-of-command as at 1 December 1995.

HQ Land Command
Operational from 1 April 1995 HQ Land Command is located at Erskine Barracks, Wilton near Salisbury and controls 72% of the troops in the British Isles and almost 100% of its fighting capability.

Land Commands's role is to deliver and sustain the Army's operational capability, whenever required throughout the world and The Command will comprise all operational troops in Great Britain, Germany, Nepal and Brunei, together with the Army Training Teams in Canada, Belize and Kenya.

Land Command comprises nearly 72,000 trained Army personnel - 72% of the Army's total, and is the largest single Top Level Budget in Defence, with a budget of just under £3 Billion (US$4.5 billion). Land Command contains all the Army's fighting equipment, including attack helicopters, Challenger 2 tanks, Warrior Infantry Fighting Vehicles, AS90 (the new artillery gun) and the Multi-Launched Rocket System (MLRS).

The Command is responsible for providing all the Army's fighting troops throughout the World. These are organised into eight formations and are commanded by Major Generals.

The Structure of Land Command

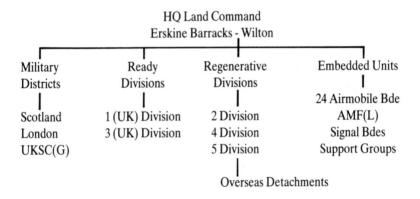

Note: Overseas Detachments include Belize, Canada, Brunei and Nepal and Kenya. Garrisons in Northern Ireland, Cyprus and the Falkland Islands are commanded from the MOD via JHQ.

Ready Divisions

There are two "Ready" Divisions: the 1st (UK) Armoured Division, based in Germany, and the 3rd (UK) Division in the United Kingdom. Both of these divisions are earmarked to form part of the Allied Command Europe Rapid Reaction Corps (ARRC), NATO's premier strategic formation; but they also have the flexibility to be employed on rapid reaction tasks or in support of other Defence Roles.

In addition to their operational roles, they also command the Army units in specified geographic areas: in the case of the 1st Division, this area is made up of the garrisons in Germany where the Division's units are based; and in the case of the 3rd Division, the South West of England.

Composition of 1(UK) Armoured Division

1 (UK) Armoured Division has its headquarters at Herford in Germany (about 50kms from Hanover) and the three Armoured Brigades under command are located at Osnabruck, Bergen-Hohne and Paderborn. The divisional personnel strength is 1,300 officers and 18,000 other ranks. Equipment totals probably resemble the following:

> 297 x Challenger MBT
> 273 x Warrior AIFV & 710 AFV 432
> 96 x AS 90 Guns and 18 x MLRS
> 24 x AVLB & 54 AAC Helicopters

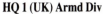
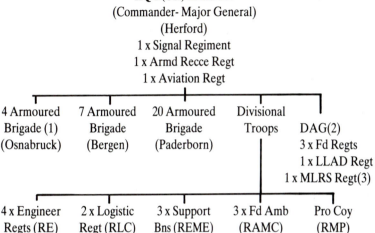

HQ 1 (UK) Armd Div
(Commander- Major General)
(Herford)
1 x Signal Regiment
1 x Armd Recce Regt
1 x Aviation Regt

| 4 Armoured Brigade (1) (Osnabruck) | 7 Armoured Brigade (Bergen) | 20 Armoured Brigade (Paderborn) | Divisional Troops | DAG(2) 3 x Fd Regts 1 x LLAD Regt 1 x MLRS Regt(3) |

| 4 x Engineer Regts (RE) | 2 x Logistic Regt (RLC) | 3 x Support Bns (REME) | 3 x Fd Amb (RAMC) | Pro Coy (RMP) |

Note: (1) Current plans appear to be for all three armoured brigades to have an identical organisation. (2) DAG (Divisional Artillery Group). This DAG could be reinforced by Rapier Air Defence and MLRS units from the UK as necessary. (3) The MLRS Regiment currently stationed in Germany is returning to the UK in late 1995. (4) Personnel total is about 19,000.

This Division could provide the Headquarters (HQs) for 12 Battlegroups.

1 (UK) Armoured Division - Armoured Brigade Organisation.

The following diagram illustrates the possible composition of an Armoured Brigade in 1(UK) Armd Div on operations.

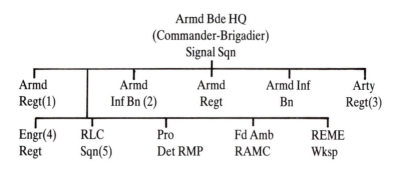

Totals: 100 x Challenger MBT (Possibly)
90 x Warrior AIFV
80 x AFV 432 APC
32 x AS 90 SP Gun
Approx 4,500 men

Notes: (1) Armoured Regiment with approx 50 Challenger MBT; (2) Armoured Inf Battalion with approx 60 x Warrior (with rifle coys) and approx 40 x FV432; (3) Artillery Regiment with 32 AS90 SP Guns; (4) Engineer Regiment with an HQ Sqn, Armd Engr Sqn, Mechanised Field Sqn and possibly additional resources dependent upon task; (5) Brigade Support Squadron RLC with approximately 60 -70 trucks; (6) Depending upon task the Brigade could expect to be reinforced with Medium Reconnaissance, Aviation and Air Defence Units.

This Brigade could provide the HQs for 4 Battlegroups

Composition of 3 (UK) Division

Following plans for the reorganisation of NATO Forces on the Central Front during 1992, the HQ of the 3rd (UK) Armoured Division moved from its old location at Soest in Germany to Bulford in Wiltshire, where it became 3(UK) Division, part of the NATO ARRC (Allied Rapid Reaction Corps). In the event of hostilities it will move to the ARRC area of operations on the European mainland or worldwide as necessary. During operations 3 (UK) Div equipment totals (excluding 3 Cdo Bde) could resemble the following: .

Main Battle Tanks (MBT) - Approx 100 x Challenger
Armoured Infantry Fighting Vehicles (AIFV) - Approx 90 x Warrior
Armoured Personnel Carriers (APCs) - Approx 172 x Saxon
Self Propelled (SP) Artillery - Approx 48 x AS90
Wheeled Artillery - Approx 18 x Light Gun
Multi Launch Rocket System (MLRS) - Approx 18 Launchers
Lynx Helicopters armed with TOW missiles - approx 24

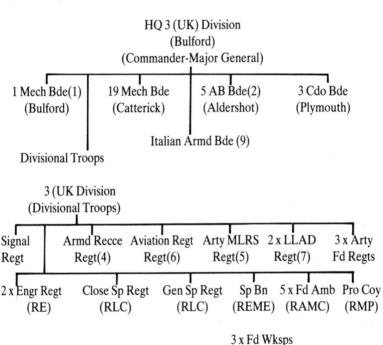

HQ 3 (UK) Division
(Bulford)
(Commander-Major General)

1 Mech Bde(1)	19 Mech Bde	5 AB Bde(2)	3 Cdo Bde
(Bulford)	(Catterick)	(Aldershot)	(Plymouth)

Italian Armd Bde (9)

Divisional Troops

3 (UK Division
(Divisional Troops)

Signal Regt	Armd Recce Regt(4)	Aviation Regt Regt(6)	Arty MLRS Regt(5)	2 x LLAD Regt(7)	3 x Arty Fd Regts

2 x Engr Regt (RE)	Close Sp Regt (RLC)	Gen Sp Regt (RLC)	Sp Bn (REME)	5 x Fd Amb (RAMC)	Pro Coy (RMP)

3 x Fd Wksps

Note: (1) 1 Mechanised Brigade; (2) 5 Airborne Brigade; (3) 3 Commando Brigade; a Royal Naval formation is available to support 3(UK) Div if necessary. Details of the organisation of 3 Cdo Bde are given in the Royal Naval Chapter. 3 Cdo Bde is not under the command of 3 (UK) Div; (4) Armoured Reconnaissance Regiment; (5) Artillery Regiment with Multi Launch Rocket System; (6) Army Air Corps Regiment with Lynx & Gazelle; (7) Air Defence Regiments with Rapier and Javelin/Starstreak missiles; (8) The composition of this division with a lightly armed parachute brigade plus a marine commando brigade allows the UK MOD to retain a balanced force for out of NATO area operations should that become necessary (9) Under Allied Rapid Reaction Corps framework agreements this division could be reinforced by an Italian Armoured Brigade (Ariete).

The Exeter based 43 Inf Bde is a reserve unit that is also under the command of 3 (UK) Division.

3 (UK) Div - Mechanised Brigade Organisation.

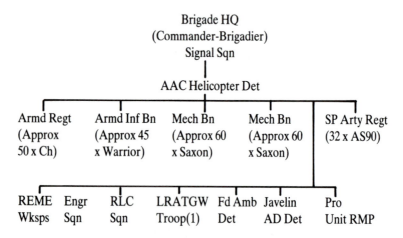

Brigade HQ
(Commander-Brigadier)
Signal Sqn

AAC Helicopter Det

Armd Regt	Armd Inf Bn	Mech Bn	Mech Bn	SP Arty Regt
(Approx 50 x Ch)	(Approx 45 x Warrior)	(Approx 60 x Saxon)	(Approx 60 x Saxon)	(32 x AS90)

REME Wksps	Engr Sqn	RLC Sqn	LRATGW Troop(1)	Fd Amb Det	Javelin AD Det	Pro Unit RMP

Note: (1) Long Range Anti-Tank Guided Weapons-Currently Striker/Swingfire.

The Battlegroup

A division usually consists of 3 brigades. These brigades are further sub-divided into smaller formations known as battlegroups. The Battlegroup is the basic building brick of the fighting formations.

A battlegroup is commanded by a Lieutenant Colonel and the infantry battalion or armoured regiment that he commands provides the command and staff element of the formation. The battlegroup is then structured according to task, with the correct mix of infantry, armour and supporting arms.

The battlegroup organisation is very flexible and the units assigned can be quickly regrouped to cope with a change in the threat. A typical battlegroup fighting a defensive battle, might be composed of one armoured squadron and two armoured infantry companies, containing about 600 men, 12 tanks and about 80 armoured personnel carriers.

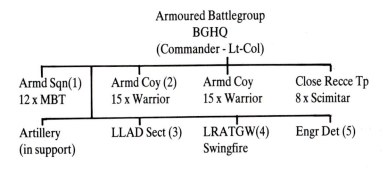

Armoured Battlegroup
BGHQ
(Commander - Lt-Col)

Armd Sqn(1) 12 x MBT	Armd Coy (2) 15 x Warrior	Armd Coy 15 x Warrior	Close Recce Tp 8 x Scimitar
Artillery (in support)	LLAD Sect (3)	LRATGW(4) Swingfire	Engr Det (5)

Mortars (in support)

(1) Armoured Squadron
(2) Armoured Infantry Company
(3) LLAD-Low Level Air Defence - Javelin
(4) LRATGW - Long Range Anti Tank Guided Weapon- Swingfire.
(5) Engineer Detachment

The number of battlegroups in a division and a brigade could vary according to the task the formation has been given. As a general rule you could expect a division to have as many as 12 battlegroups and a brigade to have up to 4.

The diagram shows a possible organisation for an armoured battlegroup in either 1(UK) Armd Div or 3(UK) Div.

Regenerative Divisions
There are three Regenerative Divisions, based on old Districts in the United Kingdom. These are the 2nd Division (replacing Eastern District) with its

Headquarters at York, the 4th Division with its Headquarters at Aldershot, and the 5th Division (replacing the old Wales and Western District) with its Headquarters at Shrewsbury. These Regenerative divisions are responsible for all Army units within their boundaries and could provide the core for three new divisions, should the Army be required to expand to meet a major international threat.

Composition of 2nd Division

The 2nd Division has responsibility for the whole of Eastern England excluding Essex. Though the Division was first formed in 1809 to fight in the Peninsular War, the crossed keys sign was not adopted until 1940 when it was reconstituted in England after Dunkirk. Its most famous engagement was during the Burma Campaign in 1944 when, at the battle for Kohima, the tide against the Japanese Army finally turned. The Divisional Headquarters is in York and the Division has two infantry brigades under command - 15 Inf Bde and 49 Inf Bde.

Composition of 4th Division

The 4th Division has military responsibility for South East England, including Bedfordshire, Essex and Hertfordshire and its headquarters is in Aldershot.
It was previously based in Germany until 1992 as an armoured division. The division now has three brigades under command - 2 Inf Bde and 145 Bde with the ARRC roled 24 Airmob Bde under command for administration and some aspects of training and operations.

Composition of 5th Division

The 5th Division has responsibility for military units and establishments in Wales, the West Midlands and the North West of England and the Headquarters is in Shrewsbury. The Division emblem, inherited from Wales and Western District, depicts the Welsh Dragon, the cross of St Chad (7th Century Bishop of Mercia), and the Red Rose of Lancaster. The Fifth Division fought at Waterloo and played a significant part in the endeavours of the BEF in both World Wars. There are three brigades under command - 42 Inf Bde, 143 Inf Bde and 160 Inf Bde.

Military Districts.

Three Districts remain: Scotland, London, and the United Kingdom Support Command (Germany). Scotland and London are responsible for all Army units within their boundaries; the United Kingdom Support Command (Germany) with its Headquarters at Rheindahlen has similar responsibilities, but also provides essential support functions for the 1st Division and the Headquarters of the ARRC.

UKSC(G)

The United Kingdom Support Command (Germany) has responsibility for British Army Troops on the Continent of Europe that are not part of 1st (United Kingdom) Armoured Division. Its headquarters replaces that of the British Army of the Rhine, whose sign it has adopted. The new headquarters is located at Rheindahlen and UKSC(G) is commanded by a Major General.

Scottish District

The Army in Scotland is commanded from a Headquarters at Craigiehall, Edinburgh which has responsibility for the entire national territory of Scotland including the Western and Northern Islands. The distinguishing flag of Army Headquarters Scotland is a Lion Rampant superimposed on a red, black and red background. The 51st Highland and the 52nd Lowland Brigades are under command.

London District

Headquarters London District was formed in 1906. It has responsibility for units that are located within the Greater London Area as well as in Windsor.

The activity for which the Headquarters and the District is most well known is State Ceremonial and Public Duties in the Capital. The district insignia shows the Sword of St Paul representing the City of London and the Mural Crown representing the County of London. The District has its Headquarters in Horse Guards.

Northern Ireland.

The military presence in Northern Ireland is commanded by HQ Northern Ireland (HQNI) siituated at Lisburn just outside Belfast and there are three Brigades under command.

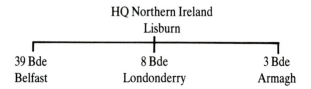

                    HQ Northern Ireland
                         Lisburn

   39 Bde   8 Bde   3 Bde
   Belfast   Londonderry   Armagh

During late 1995 under the operational command of these brigades were:

> 6 x Resident Infantry Battalions
> 3 x Infantry Battalions on short 6 month tours
> 1 x Engineer Regiment
> 1 x Royal Signals Regiment
> 1 x Army Air Corps Regiment
> 6 x Home Service Battalions of the Royal Irish Regiment
> 1 x RLC Logistic Support Regiment
> 1 x REME Workshop
> 1 x Military Hospital manned by the Army Medical Services
> 1 x Prison Guard Force of Squadron/Battery strength

RAF: 1 x Wessex Squadron; 1 x Puma Squadron
      1 x RAF Regiment Squadron

Navy: 4 x PatrolVessels
      2 x Lunches

If the recent cease-fire holds the number of units will almost certainly reduced.

Embedded Formations.

Embedded into this Land Command structure are all the other force elements which represent Land Command's operational capability. They include:

24 Airmobile Brigade, based in Colchester which is part of the Multi-National Division (Centre), an airmobile division with its headquarters in Rheindahlen.

Three signal Brigades (one of which is in Germany).

Two Combat Service Support Groups (one of which is in Germany).

Various additional units which are earmarked for the ACE Rapid Reaction Corps or for National Defence tasks.

The overseas detachments in Canada, Belize, Brunei and Nepal are commanded directly from Headquarters Land Command at Wilton.

The United Kingdom element of the ACE Mobile Force (Land).

Allied Command Europe Mobile Force Land AMF(L) Contingent that is the UK's contribution to the Allied Command Europe Mobile Force (AMF) which is tasked with the reinforcement of the flanks of NATO. On mobilisation operations would probably take place in either Norway or Turkey and the UK MOD has recently stated that the UK's contribution to the AMF will be retained. The AMF is a Brigade+ NATO formation with about 6,000 men and 1,500 vehicles. The UK AMF(L) has its Headquarters and logistic elements at Bulford and an infantry battalion at Dover.

24 Airmobile Brigade (24 Airmob Bde).

On 1 April 1988, 24 Infantry Brigade based at Catterick in North Yorkshire, was redesignated 24 Airmobile Brigade with the role of acting as a flexible, high speed anti-tank reserve force. The Brigade moved to Colchester in March 1993, and was enhanced considerably under the "Options for Change" review. 24 Airmob Bde now forms part of the Multi National Division - Central (MND(C)) which was formed officially on 1 April 1994. The MND(C) also comprises 31 German Luftlande Brigade, a Belgian Paracommando Brigade and 11 Netherlands Airmobile Brigade, giving the Division the reach, speed and flexibility it will require to be part of the ARRC's most mobile formation.

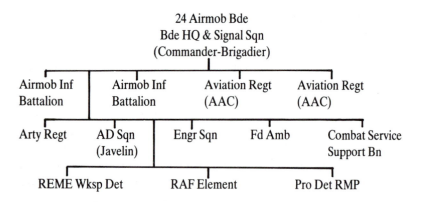

24 Airmob Bde
Bde HQ & Signal Sqn
(Commander-Brigadier)

| Airmob Inf Battalion | Airmob Inf Battalion | Aviation Regt (AAC) | Aviation Regt (AAC) |

| Arty Regt | AD Sqn (Javelin) | Engr Sqn | Fd Amb | Combat Service Support Bn |

| REME Wksp Det | RAF Element | Pro Det RMP |

Note: (1) Support helicopters are provided by the RAF and the Brigade would normally expect to operate with 18 x Chinook and 18 x Puma. An airmobile infantry battalion can be moved by 20 x Chinook equivalents. (2) Each airmobile infantry battalion is equipped with 42 x Milan firing posts - a total of 84 within the Brigade.(3) By late 1995 plus we believe that 3 Regt Army Air Corps and 4 Regt Army Air Corps both of whom will be based at RAF Wattisham will support 24 Airmob Bde. During mid 1995 units of the Brigade moved to the former Yugoslavia for operations in support of UNPROFOR.

Units of the Army.

The Cavalry.

Apart from the Royal Tank Regiment, which was formed in the First World War with the specific task of fighting in armoured vehicles, tank forces in the British Army are provided by the regiments which formed the cavalry element of the pre-mechanised era. Following the "Options for Change" restructuring in January 1995 there were 11 regular armoured regiments and 5 TA armoured regiments. One of these regiments forms The Household Cavalry and the remaining regiments are known collectively as The Royal Armoured Corps (RAC).

Of these 11 regular armoured regiments, 7 are stationed in Germany with 1 (UK) Armoured Division, and of these 7 regiments in 1 (UK) Armoured Division - 6 are equipped with Challenger 1/2 main battle tanks, and the 7th is an armoured reconnaissance regiment equipped with a mix of Scimitar, Striker and Spartan.

In the UK there are 2 regular armoured regiments equipped with Challenger MBT stationed in Tidworth and Catterick. Both of these regiments are under the operational command of 3 (UK) Division that has a role in support of the ARRC. There is also 1 regular armoured reconnaissance regiment stationed in the UK also under the operational command of 3 (UK) Division. An armoured training regiment is based at the RAC Training Centre located at Bovington in Dorset. In addition to these armoured forces the Household Cavalry Mounted Regiment is stationed in London and provides mounted troops for ceremonial duties.

The Territorial Army has 5 Yeomanry Regiments and an independent squadron. These units provide 1 armoured reconnaissance regiment for the reinforcement of the ARRC and 4 national defence regiments with a reconnaissance role.

The Cavalry accounts for about 6% of the strength of the Army and Regimental Titles are as follows:

The Household Cavalry.

The Household Cavalry Regiment	HCR
The Household Cavalry Mounted Regiment	HCMRD

The Royal Armoured Corps

1st The Queen's Dragoon Guards	QDG
The Royal Scots Dragoon Guards	SCOTS DG
The Royal Dragoon Guards	RDG
The Queen's Royal Hussars	QRH
9th/12th Royal Lancers	9/12L
The King's Royal Hussars	KRH
The Light Dragoons	LD
The Queen's Royal Lancers	QRL
1st Royal Tank Regiment	1 RTR
2nd Royal Tank Regiment	2 RTR

Permanent Locations:

| United Kingdom | - | 4 Regiments |
| Germany | - | 7 Regiments |

Armoured Regiment Wiring Diagram

The following diagram shows the current structure of an Armoured Regiment equipped with Challenger 1. Regiments equipped with Challenger 2 will only have three "sabre" squadrons and a total of 38 tanks.

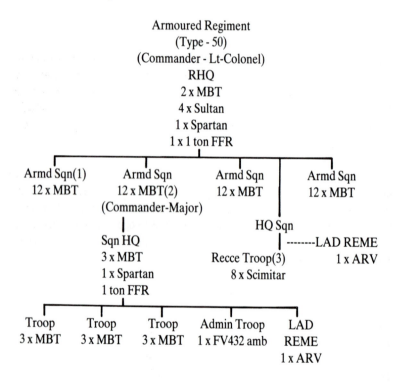

Totals: 50 x MBT (Challenger 1), 8 x Scimitar, 5 x ARV, 558 men.

Notes: (1) Armoured Squadron; (2) Main Battle Tank (3) We believe that this recce troop of 8 x Scimitar is normally held in HQ Sqn but on operations comes under the direct control of the commanding officer (4) By late 1993 all 6 regiments in Germany with 1(UK) Armd Div were equipped with Challenger. (5) The basic building brick of the Tank Regiment is the Tank Troop of 12 men and three tanks. The commander of this troop will probably be a Lt or 2/Lt aged between 20 or 23 and the second-in-command will usually be a sergeant who commands his own tank. The remaining tank in the troop will be commanded by a senior corporal (6) A Challenger tank has a crew of 4 - Commander, Driver, Gunner and Loader/Operator.

The Infantry

The British Infantry is based on the well tried and tested Regimental System that has been justified regularly on operational deployment, it is based on battalions, which when they number more than one are grouped together to form a "large Regiment". Most Regiments now comprise one Regular and one TA battalion and Regiments are then grouped together within Divisions, which provide a level of administrative command.

The Division of Infantry is an organisation that is responsible for all aspects of military administration, from recruiting, manning and promotions for individuals in the regiments under its wing, to the longer term planning required to ensure continuity and cohesion. Divisions of Infantry have no operational command over their regiments, and should not be confused with the operational divisions such as 1(UK) Armd Div and 3(UK) Div.

The Divisions of Infantry are as follows:

The Guards Division	- 5 regular battalions
The Scottish Division	- 6 regular battalions
The Queen's Division	- 6 regular battalions
The King's Division	- 6 regular battalions
The Prince of Wales Division	- 7 regular battalions
The Light Division	- 4 regular battalions.

Not administered by Divisions of Infantry but operating under their own administrative arrangements are the following:

The Parachute Regiment	- 3 regular battalions
The Brigade of Gurkhas	- 3 regular battalions
The Royal Irish Regiment	- 1 regular battalion

With the exception of the Guards Division and the Brigade of Gurkhas, all the infantry divisional organisations listed have a varying number of the 36 TA battalions in the British Infantry under their administrative control. In total the British Army will have 41 regular battalions available for service and this total combined with the 36 TA battalions could give a mobilisation strength of 77 infantry battalions (late 1995). Following the announcement of changes in the organisation of the TA, we believe that this total will be reduced and that in the future there will be 29 TA infantry battalions and 4 TA fire support battalions available.

The Infantry accounts for about 25% of the Army which, after the latest reorganisation will be divided into 41 general service battalions, plus six battalions of The Royal Irish Regiment which will be used only in Northern Ireland and The Special Air Service Regiment. The British Infantry is organised as follows:

The Guards Division

1st Bn The Grenadier Guards	1 GREN GDS
1st Bn The Coldstream Guards	1 COLM GDS
1st Bn The Scots Guards	1 SG
1st Bn The Irish Guards	1 IG
1st Bn The Welsh Guards	1 WG

There are generally three battalions from the Guards Division on public duties in London at any one time. When a Regiment is stationed in London on public duties it is given an extra company to ensure the additional manpower required for ceremonial events is available. The 2nd Bns of the Grenadier, Coldstream and Scots Guards have been placed in suspended animation.

The Scottish Division

1st Bn The Royal Scots	1 RS
1st Bn The Royal Highland Fusiliers	1 RHF
1st Bn The King's Own Scottish Borderers	1 KOSB
1st Bn The Black Watch	1 BW
1st Bn The Argyll & Sutherland Highlanders	1 A & SH
1st Bn The Highlanders	1 HLDRS

The Queen's Division

1st Bn The Priness of Wales' Royal Regiment (Queen's and Royal Hampshire)	1 PWRR
2nd Bn The Princess of Wales's Royal Regiment (Queen's and Royal Hampshire)	2 PWRR
1st Bn The Royal Regiment of Fusiliers	1 RRF
2nd Bn The Royal Regiment of Fusiliers	2 RRF
1st Bn The Royal Anglian Regiment	1 R ANGLIAN
2nd Bn The Royal Anglian Regiment	2 R ANGLIAN

The King's Division

1st Bn The King's Own Royal Border Regiment	1 KINGS OWN BORDER
1st Bn The King's Regiment	1 KINGS
1st Bn The Prince of Wales's Own Regiment of Yorkshire	1 PWO
1st Bn The Green Howards	1 GREEN HOWARDS
1st Bn The Queen's Lancashire Regiment	1 QLR
1st Bn The Duke of Wellington's Regiment	1 DWR

The Prince of Wales Division

1st Bn The Devonshire & Dorset Regiment	1 D and D
1st Bn The Cheshire Regiment	1 CHESHIRE
1st Bn The Royal Welch Fusiliers	1 RWF
1st Bn The Royal Regiment of Wales	1 RRW
1st Bn The Royal Gloucestershire, Wiltshire and Berkshire Regiment	1 RGWBR
1st Bn The Worcestershire & Sherwood Foresters Regiment	1 WFR

1st Bn The Staffordshire Regiment	1 STAFFORDS

The Light Division

1st Bn The Light Infantry	1 LI
2nd Bn The Light Infantry	2 LI
1st Bn The Royal Green Jackets	1 RGJ
2nd Bn The Royal Green Jackets	2 RGJ

The Brigade of Gurkhas

1st Bn The Royal Gurkha Regiment	1 RGR
2nd Bn The Royal Gurkha Regiment	2 RGR
3rd Bn The Royal Gurkha Regiment	3 RGR

In 1996/97 2 RGR and 3 RGR will amalgamate to form 2 RGR leaving only two Gurkha battalions in the Army - 1 RGR and 2 RGR. Gurkha Recruits are trained at Church Crookham in Hampshire under the wing of the resident UK Gurkha Battalion.

The Parachute Regiment

1st Bn The Parachute Regiment	1 PARA
2nd Bn The Parachute Regiment	2 PARA
3rd Bn The Parachute Regiment	3 PARA

The Royal Irish Regiment

1st Bn The Royal Irish Regiment	1 R IRISH
3rd/4th/5th/7th/8th/9th Royal Irish Regiment*	3-9 R IRISH

* The 3rd to 8th Bns The Royal Irish Regiment are employed exclusively in Northern Ireland and were formerly battalions of The Ulster Defence Regiment. The 4/5 Rangers is a TA Battalion stationed in Northern Ireland and wearing the Royal Irish capbadge.

Infantry Battalions - Permanent Locations

United Kingdom	-	31 Battalions
Germany	-	6 Battalions
Cyprus	-	2 Battalions

| Hong Kong | - | 1 Battalion |
| Brunei | - | 1 Battalion |

The Special Air Service Regiment
The 22nd Special Air Service Regiment 22 SAS.

The SAS can be classed as an infantry unit but the members of the regiment are found from all arms and services of the Army after exhaustive selection tests.

Infantry Organisations

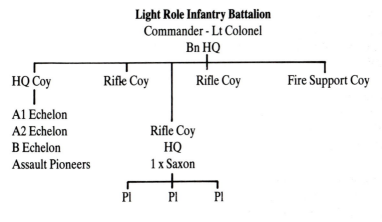

Light Role Infantry Battalion
Commander - Lt Colonel
Bn HQ

HQ Coy   Rifle Coy   Rifle Coy   Fire Support Coy

A1 Echelon
A2 Echelon   Rifle Coy
B Echelon   HQ
Assault Pioneers   1 x Saxon

Pl   Pl   Pl

Totals
6 x Milan
9 x 81mm Mortars
624 All Ranks

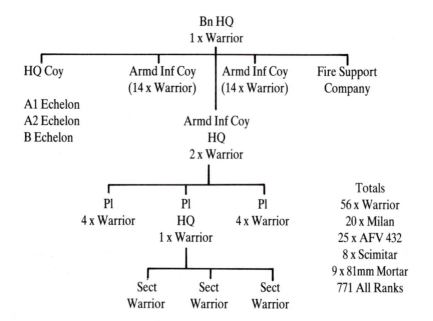

Armoured Infantry Battalion
Commander - Lt Colonel

Bn HQ
1 x Warrior

HQ Coy

A1 Echelon
A2 Echelon
B Echelon

Armd Inf Coy
(14 x Warrior)

Armd Inf Coy
(14 x Warrior)

Fire Support
Company

Armd Inf Coy
HQ
2 x Warrior

Pl
4 x Warrior

Pl
HQ
1 x Warrior

Pl
4 x Warrior

Sect
Warrior

Sect
Warrior

Sect
Warrior

Totals
56 x Warrior
20 x Milan
25 x AFV 432
8 x Scimitar
9 x 81mm Mortar
771 All Ranks

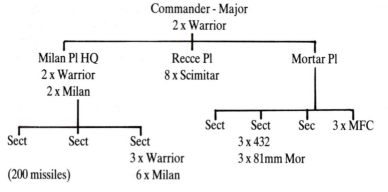

Armoured Infantry Battalion - Fire Support Company
Commander - Major
2 x Warrior

Milan Pl HQ
2 x Warrior
2 x Milan

Recce Pl
8 x Scimitar

Mortar Pl

Sect

Sect

Sect
3 x Warrior
6 x Milan

(200 missiles)

Sect

Sect

Sec
3 x 432
3 x 81mm Mor

3 x MFC

Note: (1) There are 8 x Armoured Infantry Battalions, 6 of which are in Germany with 1 (UK) Armoured Division and the remaining 2 in the UK with 3 (UK) Division. (2) There are longer term intentions to replace the AFV 432s on issue to armoured infantry battalions by other versions of Warrior or equivalent vehicles such as mortar carrier, ambulance, command vehicle etc.(3) Another 4 Milan firing posts are held by the mobilisation section that is only activated in war.

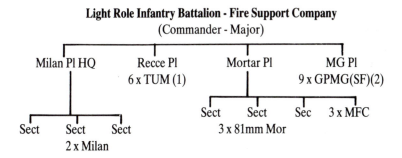

Light Role Infantry Battalion - Fire Support Company
(Commander - Major)

Notes: (1) TUM is the abbreviation for Truck-Utility-Medium; (2) General Purpose Machine Guns mounted on tripods with a range of up to 1,800 metres.

The Royal Regiment of Artillery   **RA**

The Royal Regiment of Artillery provides the battlefield fire support and air defence for the British Army in the field. Its various regiments are equipped for conventional fire support using field guns, for area and point air defence using air defence missiles and for specialised artillery locating tasks. By September 1990 the first Regiment equipped with the Multiple Launch Rocket System (MLRS) had taken its place in the Order of Battle and these weapons were used with great effect during the war in the Gulf.

By late 1995 the RA, one of the larger organisations in the British Army with 16 Regiments included in its Order of Battle, will have the following structure in both the UK and Germany (ARRC).

	UK	Germany
Field Regiments (AS 90 SP Guns)	2	3
Field Regiments (FH70 or Light Gun)	3(1)	-

Depth Fire Regiments (MLRS)	3	-
Air Defence Regiments (Rapier)	2	1
Air Defence Regiment (HVM)	1	-
Training Regiment	1	-
The Kings Troop (Ceremonial)	1	-

Note: (1) Of these 3 Regiments 1 is a Commando Regiment (29 Cdo Regt) and another a Parachute Regiment (7 RHA). (2) Although the artillery is organised into Regiments, much of a "gunner's" loyalty is directed towards the battery in which he serves. A Regiment will generally have three or four batterys under command. Following "Options for Change" by late 1994 the Artillery will have reduced from 23 Regiments (76 titled batterys) to 16 Regiments (56 titled batterys). The Royal Horse Artillery (RHA) is also part of the Royal Regiment of Artillery and its three regiments have been included in the totals above. There is considerable cross posting of officers and soldiers from the RA to the RHA, and some consider service with the RHA to be a career advancement.

Artillery training is carried out at the Royal School of Artillery at Larkhill in Wiltshire. After initial training officers and gunners will be posted to RA units world-wide, but soldiers will return to the RSA for frequent career and employment courses. Artillery recruits spend the first period of recruit training (Common Military Syllabus) at the Army Training Regiment - Litchfield.

Air Defence is a vital part of the role of the Royal Artillery and updates to the Rapier system continue, and batterys being upgraded to Field Standard B2 and Field Standard C. During 1994 a Starstreak HVM Regiment became operational in the UK. In addition, the air defences will be enhanced by the Air Defence Alerting Device for Javelin and Starstreak, and the Air Defence Command, Control and Information System entered service during late 1994.

The Royal Artillery provides the modern British armoured formation with a protective covering. The air defence covers the immediate airspace above and around the formation, with the field artillery reaching out to approximately 30kms in front and across the flanks of the formation. An armoured formation that moves out of this protective covering is open to immediate destruction by an intelligent enemy as the Egyptians discovered in 1973.

Divisional Artillery Group (DAG)
An armoured or mechanised division has it own artillery under command. This artillery usually consists of 3 Close Support Regiments, with a number of units detached from the Corps Artillery and could include TA reinforcements.

In war the composition of the DAG will vary according to the task.
The following is a diagram of the artillery support available to 1(UK) Armd Div deployed with the ARRC in Germany. Expect each brigade in the division to have one Close Support Regiment with AS90 under command.

The number of batterys and final number of guns per battery in an AS90 Close Support Regiment appears to have been finally resolved at 4 batterys of eight guns per battery to enable the 4 battlegroups in each brigade to be fully supported. Although a battery has eight gun on establishment only six guns will be manned in peacetime.

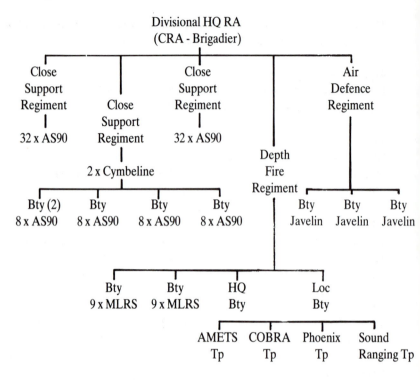

Notes:

(1) Air defended areas (ADAs) are provided by Rapier. There is one Rapier Regiment in Germany and one in the UK.

(2) We expect all AS90 deliveries to be complete during 1996.

(3) The Staff of an armoured or mechanised division includes a Brigadier of Artillery known as the Commander Royal Artillery (CRA). The CRA acts as the artillery advisor to the Divisional Commander, and would probably assign one of his Close Support Regiments to support each of the Brigades in the division. These regiments would be situated in positions that would allow most of their batterys to fire across the complete divisional front.

Therefore, in the very best case, a battlegroup under extreme threat could be supported by the fire of more than 96 guns.

Royal Artillery Regiments

1st Regiment Royal Horse Artillery	1 RHA	(Field)
3rd Regiment Royal Horse Artillery	3 RHA	(Field)
4th Regiment	4 REGT	(Field)
5th Regiment	5 REGT	(MLRS)
7th Regiment Royal Horse Artillery	7 RHA	(Parachute)
12th Regiment	12 REGT	(Air Defence)
14th Regiment	14 REGT	(Training)
16th Regiment	16 REGT	(Air Defence)
19th Regiment	19 REGT	(Field)
22nd Regiment	22 REGT	(Air Defence)
26th Regiment	26 REGT	(Field)
29th Commando Regiment	29 REGT	(Field)
32nd Regiment	32 REGT	(MLRS)
39th Regiment	39 REGT	(MLRS)
40th Regiment	40 REGT	(Field)
47th Regiment	47 REGT	(Air Defence)

Army Air Corps

The Army obtains its aviation support from the Army Air Corps (AAC), which is an Army organisation with 5 separate regiments and a number of independent squadrons. The AAC also provides support for Northern Ireland on a mixed resident and roulement basis and the two squadrons concerned are sometimes referred to as the sixth AAC Regiment, although the units would disperse on mobilisation and have no regimental title. By mid 1995 and following the "Options for Change" restructuring AAC regimental locations will be as follows:

1 Regiment	-	Germany
3 Regiment	-	Wattisham
4 Regiment	-	Wattisham
7 Regiment	-	Netheravon
9 Regiment	-	Dishforth

In addition to the Regiments in the UK and Germany there are small flights in Cyprus, Suffield (Canada) and the Falkland Islands. In Hong Kong 660 Sqn has 10 aircraft with a small detachment in Brunei.

The AAC Centre at Middle Wallop in Hampshire acts as a focal point for all Army Aviation, and it is here that the majority of training for pilots and aircrew is carried out.

Although the AAC operates some fixed wing aircraft for training, liaison flying and radar duties, the main effort goes into providing helicopter support for the ground forces. About 350 AAC helicopters are used for anti-tank operations, artillery fire control, reconnaissance, liaison flying and a limited troop lift. In July 1995 the UK MoD announced the purchase of 67 x Longbow Apache attack helicopters that will be licence manufactured in the UK by Westland Helicopters.

Army Air Corps - Regimental Designations

1st Regiment	1 REGT AAC
3rd Regiment	3 REGT AAC
4th Regiment	4 REGT AAC
7th Regiment	7 REGT AAC
9th Regiment	9 REGT AAC

AAC Regimental Organisation

Organisations for the individual AAC Regiments appear to be in a state of flux. The following wiring diagram outlines the organisation of a 3 Regiment AAC in early 1995. 3 Regiment AAC supports the Colchester based 24 Airmobile Brigade and various regimental organisations are a variation on this theme.

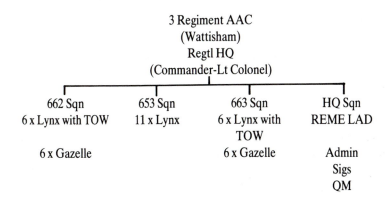

3 Regiment AAC
(Wattisham)
Regtl HQ
(Commander-Lt Colonel)

662 Sqn	653 Sqn	663 Sqn	HQ Sqn
6 x Lynx with TOW	11 x Lynx	6 x Lynx with TOW	REME LAD
6 x Gazelle		6 x Gazelle	Admin
			Sigs
			QM

Totals: Approx 450 personnel
35 Helicopters

(1) A Regiment of this type could act as the core formation of an airborne battlegroup. If necessary an infantry aviation company consisting of 3 x rifle platoons and a Milan anti-tank platoon will be attached. The infantry could be moved in RAF Chinooks or Pumas.

(2) 4 Regiment AAC joined 3 Regiment in Wattisham during early 1995 and we believe that both regiments will have a similar organisation. Wattisham is also the home of 7 Bn REME - a unit configured as an aircraft workshops.

Westland Longbow Apache shortly to be on issue to the Army Air Corps (Westland Helicopters).

A 227mm MLRS of 1 UK Armoured Division moves into position at Sennelager in Germany (P Info BFG).

TA soldiers of 4 Para (Leeds) undergoing live fire training at Otterburn (P Info 2 Div).

A light strike vehicle of 24 Airmobile Brigade (P Info 2 Div).

Corps of Royal Engineers

The engineer support for the Army is provided by the Corps of Royal Engineers (RE). This large corps, currently composed of 19 regiments filled with highly skilled tradesmen is currently organised as follows:

	Germany	UKLF
Engineer Regiments	4	4
EOD Regiment	-	1
Resident N Ireland Regiment	-	1
TA Engineer Regiments	-	9

There are also a number of independent engineer squadrons world-wide.

The Royal Engineers provide specialist support to the combat formations and engineer detachments can be found at all levels from the Combat Team/Company Group upwards. Combat Engineers tasks are amongst the following:

a. **Defence**: Construction of field defences; minelaying; improvement and construction of obstacles.
b. **Attack**: Obstacle crossing; demolition of enemy defences (bunkers etc); mine clearance; bridge or ferry construction.
c. **Advance**: Building or strengthening roads and bridges; removal of booby traps; mine clearance; airfield construction; supply of water; survey.
d. **Withdrawal**: Demolition - of airfields, roads and bridges, fuel ammunition and fooddumps, railway tracks and rolling stock,industrial plant and facilities such as power stations; route clearance; minelaying; booby trapping likely enemy future positions and items that might be attractive to the enemy. Often amongst the first soldiers into battle, and still involved in dangerous tasks such as mine clearance in the former Yugoslavia, the Sappers can turn their hands to almost any engineering task.

Recent UN tasks have highlighted the importance of combat engineers. Tasks for which engineer support was requested stretched the resources of the Corps to its limit and the first priority in almost any call from the UN for support is for engineers. Tracks have to be improved, roads must be built, wells dug and clean water provided together with camps for refugees All of these are engineer tasks that soak up large amounts of manpower.

Engineer Organisations

The smallest engineer unit is the field troop which is usually commanded by a Lieutenant and consists of approximately 44 men. In an armoured division a field troop can be expect to have up to four sections and each section is mounted in an APC. Engineer Regiments in UKLF may have only three sections and may be mounted in wheeled vehicles such as Land Rovers and 4 Ton Trucks. An engineer troop will carry equipment, stores and explosives to enable it to carry out its immediate battlefield tasks.

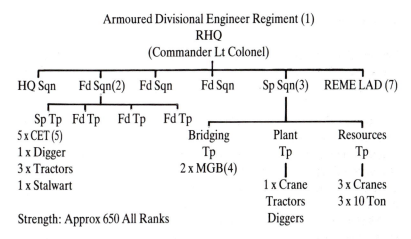

Armoured Divisional Engineer Regiment (1)
RHQ
(Commander Lt Colonel)

| HQ Sqn | Fd Sqn(2) | Fd Sqn | Fd Sqn | Sp Sqn(3) | REME LAD (7) |

Sp Tp   Fd Tp   Fd Tp   Fd Tp

	Bridging	Plant	Resources
5 x CET (5)	Tp	Tp	Tp
1 x Digger	2 x MGB(4)		
3 x Tractors		1 x Crane	3 x Cranes
1 x Stalwart		Tractors	3 x 10 Ton
Strength: Approx 650 All Ranks		Diggers	

(1) This Regiment would send most of its soldiers to man the engineer detachments that provide support for a division's battlegroups; (2) Field Squadron (expect a field squadron to have approximately 68 vehicles and some 200 men; (3) Support Squadron; (4) Medium Girder Bridge; (5) Combat Engineer Tractor; (6) This whole organisation is highly mobile and built around the AFV 432 and Spartan series of vehicles; (7) In addition to the regimental REME LAD each squadron has its own REME section of approximately 12 - 15 men.

Engineer amphibious capability and specialist support is provided by elements of 28 Engineer Regiment in Germany and a TA Regiment in the UK.

The UK Engineer Field Regiment (Regular & TA) is generally a wheeled organisation that might be expected to have 2 Field Squadrons, a Support Squadron and possibly an Airfield Damage Repair (ADR) Squadron. Engineer regiments supporting 3(UK) Division could be structured along the lines of the Armoured Divisional Engineer Regiment.

Royal Engineers - Regimental Designations

1st RSME Regiment	1 RSME REGT RE
3rd RSME Regiment	3 RSME REGT RE
21st Engineer Regiment	21 ENGR REGT
22nd Engineer Regiment	22 ENGR REGT
25th Engineer Regiment	25 ENGR REGT
28th ngineer Regiment	28 ENR REGT
32nd Engineer Regiment	32 ARMD ENGR REGT
33rd Engineer Regiment	33 ENGR REGT (EOD)
35th Engineer Regiment	35 ENGR REGT
36th Engineer Regiment	36 ENGR REGT
38th Engineer Regiment	38 ENGR REGT
39th Engineer Regiment	39 ENGR REGT

The total for the UK includes the 2 x RSME Training Regiments.

The Royal Corps of Signals

The Royal Corps of Signals (R Signals) provides the communications throughout the command system of the Army. Individual battlegroups are responsible for their own internal communications, but all communications from Brigade level and above are the responsibility of the Royal Signals.

Information is the life-blood of any military formation in battle and it is the responsibility of the Royal Signals to ensure the speedy and accurate passage of information that enables commanders to make informed and timely decisions, and to ensure that those decisions are passed to the fighting troops in contact with the enemy. The rapid, accurate and secure employment of command, control and communications systems maximises the effect of the military force available and consequently the Royal Signals acts as an extremely significant 'Force Multiplier'.

The Royal Corps of Signals provides about 9% of the Army's manpower with 11 Regular and 11 Territorial Army Regiments, each generally consisting of between 3 and up to 6 Sqns with between 400 and 1,000 personnel. In addition, there are 20 Regular and 2 Territorial Army Independent Squadrons, each of which has about 200 men, and 4 Independent Signal Troops of between 10 and 80 men each. Royal Signals personnel are found wherever the Army is deployed including every UK and NATO headquarters in the world. The Headquarters of the Corps is at the Royal School of Signals (RSS) located at Blandford in Dorset.

Royal Signals units based in the United Kingdom provide command, control and communications for forces that have operational roles both in the UK itself, including Northern Ireland, and overseas including mainland Western Europe and further afield wherever the Army finds itself. There are a number of Royal Signals units permanently based in Germany, Holland and Belgium from where they provide the necessary command and control communications and Electronic Warfare (EW) support for both the British Army and other NATO forces based in Europe. Royal Signals units are also based in Cyprus, Hong Kong, the Falkland Islands, Belize and Gibraltar.

Armoured Divisional Signal Regiment Organisation

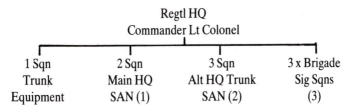

Notes: (1) SAN - Secondary Access Node (2) A Divisional HQ will have two HQs to allow for movement and possible destruction. The main HQ will be set up for approx 24 hrs with the alternate HQ (Alt HQ) set up 20-30 kms away on the proposed line of march of the division. When the Main HQ closes to move to a new location the Alt HQ becomes the Main HQ for another 24 hour period. (3) Expect a Brigade Sig Sqn to have a Radio Troop and a SAN Troop.

The Royal Logistic Corps (RLC)

The RLC is the youngest Corps in the Army and was formed in April 1993 as a result of the recommendations of the MoD's Logistic Support Review. The RLC results from the amalgamation of the Royal Corps of Transport (RCT), the Royal Army Ordnance Corps (RAOC), the Army Catering Corps (ACC), the Royal Pioneer Corps (RPC) and elements of the Royal Enginers (RE). The Corps makes up about 16% of the Army with 20,000 Regular soldiers and 10,000 Territorial Army soldiers wearing its cap badge.

The RLC has very broad responsibilities throughout the Army including the movement of personnel throughout the world, the Army's air dispatch service, maritime and rail transport, operational resupply, explosive ordnance disposal which includes the hazardous bomb disposal duties in Northern Ireland and in mainland Britain during the recent IRA terrorist campaign, the operation of numerous very large vehicle and stores depots both in the UK and overseas, the training and provision of cooks to virtually all units in the Army, the provision of pioneer labour and the Army's postal and courier service.

The principle field elements of the RLC are the Close Support and the General Support Regiments whose primary role is to supply the fighting units with ammunition, fuel and rations (Combat Supplies).

A division has an integral Close Support Regiment which is responsible for manning and operating the supply chain to Brigades and Divisional units.

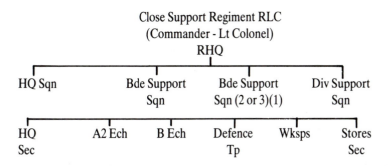

Close Support Regiment RLC
(Commander - Lt Colonel)
RHQ

- HQ Sqn
- Bde Support Sqn
- Bde Support Sqn (2 or 3)(1)
- Div Support Sqn
  - HQ Sec
  - A2 Ech
  - B Ech
  - Defence Tp
  - Wksps
  - Stores Sec

Note: (1) A regiment could have two or three brigade support sqns depending upon the size of the division being supported. (2) Some of these regiments may have a Postal and Courier Sqn.

The General Support Regiment's role is primarily to supply ammunition to the Royal Artillery using DROPS vehicles and to provide Tank Transporters that move armoured vehicles more rapidly and economically than moving them on their own tracks.

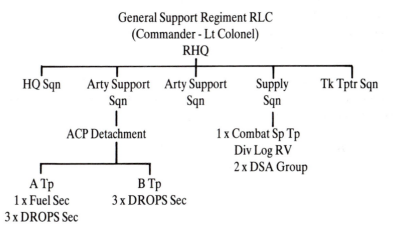

General Support Regiment RLC
(Commander - Lt Colonel)
RHQ

- HQ Sqn
- Arty Support Sqn
  - ACP Detachment
    - A Tp
      1 x Fuel Sec
      3 x DROPS Sec
    - B Tp
      3 x DROPS Sec
- Arty Support Sqn
- Supply Sqn
  - 1 x Combat Sp Tp
    Div Log RV
    2 x DSA Group
- Tk Tptr Sqn

Both types of Regiment have large sections holding stores both on wheels and on the ground. A Division will typically require about 1,000 tons of Combat Supplies a day but demand can easily exceed that amount in high intensity operations.

The Royal Electrical & Mechanical Engineers (REME)

The Logistic Support review of 1990 recommended that Equipment Support should remain separate from the other logistic pillar of Service Support and consequently the REME has retained not only its own identity but expanded its responsibilities. Equipment Support encompasses equipment management, engineering support, supply management, provisioning for vehicle and technical spares and financial management responsibilities for in-service equipment.

The aim of the REME is "To keep operationally fit equipment in the hands of the troops" and in the current financial environment it is important that this is carried out at the minimum possible cost. The equipment that REME is responsible for ranges from small arms and trucks to helicopters and Main Battle Tanks. All field force units have some integral REME support which will vary, depending on the size of the unit and the equipment held, from a few attached tradesmen up to a large Regimental Workshop of over 200 men. In war REME is responsible for the recovery and repair of battle damaged and unserviceable equipments.

The development of highly technical weapon systems and other equipment has meant that REME has had to balance engineering and tactical considerations.
On the one hand the increased scope for forward repair of equipment reduces the time out of action, but on the other hand engineering stability is required for the repair of complex systems. The major changes which have resulted from the Options for Change and Logistic Support Reviews are that four REME battalions were formed in 1993, to provide second line support for the British contribution to the ACE Rapid Reaction Corps (ARRC).

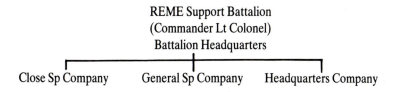

REME Support Battalion
(Commander Lt Colonel)
Battalion Headquarters

Close Sp Company   General Sp Company   Headquarters Company

FRGs & MRGs

Note: Approx 450 personnel. At the beginning of 1995 there were 5 Regular
REME Support battalions, 3 in Germany and 2 in the UK.

The Close Support Company will normally deploy a number of FRG's (Forward
Repair Groups) and MRGs (Medium Repair Groups) in support of brigades. The
company is mobile with armoured repair and recovery vehicles able to operate in
the forward areas, carrying out forward repair of key nominated equipment often
by the exchange of major assemblies. It is also capable of carrying out field
repairs on priority equipment including telecommunications equipment and the
repair of damage sustained by critical battle winning equipments.

The role of the General Support Company is to support the Close Support
Companies and Divisional Troops. Tasks include the regeneration of fit power
packs for use in forward repair and the repair of equipment backloaded from
Close Support Companies. The General Support Company will normally be
located to the rear of the divisional area in order to maximise productivity and
minimise vulnerability.

Army Medical Services

Royal Army Medical Corps
In peace, the personnel of the RAMC are based at the various medical
installations throughout the world or in field force units and they are responsible
for the health of the Army.

The primary role of the Corps is the maintenance of health and the prevention of
disease. On operations, the RAMC is responsible for the care of the sick and
wounded, with the subsequent evacuation of the wounded to hospitals in the rear

areas. Each Brigade has a field ambulance which is a regular unit that operates in direct support of the battlegroups. These units are either armoured, airmobile or parachute trained. In addition each division has two field ambulance units regular or TA that provide medical support for the divisional troops and can act as manoeuvre units for the forward brigades when required.

All field ambulance units have medical sections that consist of a medical officer and eight Combat Medical Technicians. These sub-units are located with the battlegroup or units being supported and they provide the necessary first line medical support. In addition, the field ambulance provides a dressing station where casualties are treated and may be resuscitated or stabilised before transfer to a field hospital. These units have the necessary integral ambulance support, both armoured and wheeled to transfer casualties from the first to second line medical units.

Field hospitals may be regular or TA and all are 200 bed facilities with a maximum of 8 surgical teams capable of carrying out life saving operations on some of the most difficult surgical cases. Since 1990 most regular medical units have been deployed on operations either in the Persian Gulf or the former Yugoslavia.

Casualty Evacuation (CASEVAC) is by either armoured or wheeled ambulance and driven by RLC personnel or even by helicopter when such aircraft are available. A Chinook helicopter is capable of carrying 44 stretcher cases and a Puma can carry 6 stretcher cases and 6 sitting cases.

The Queen Alexandra's Royal Army Nursing Corps (QARANC)
On the 1st April 1992 the QARANC became an all-nursing and totally professionally qualified Corps. Its male and female, officer and other rank personnel, provide the necessary qualified nursing support at all levels and covering a wide variety of nursing specialities. QARANC personnel can be found anywhere in the world where Army Medical services are required.

Royal Army Dental Corps (RADC)
The RADC is a professional corps that in late 1994 consisted of just over 400 officers and soldiers. The Corps fulfils the essential role of maintaining the dental health of the Army in peace and war, both at home and overseas.
Qualified dentists and oral surgeons, hygienists, technicians and support ancillaries work in a wide variety of military units - from static and mobile dental clinics to field medical units, military hospitals and dental laboratories.

The Adjutant General's Corps (AGC)
The Adjutant General's Corps formed on 1 April 1992 and its sole task is the management of the Army's personnel. The Corps absorbed the functions of six existing smaller corps; the Royal Military Police, the Royal Army Pay Corps, the Royal Army Educational Corps, the Royal Army Chaplains Department, the Army Legal Corps and the Military Provost Staff Corps.

The Corps is organised into four branches, Staff and Personnel Support, Provost, Educational and Training Services and Army Legal Services. By 1995, after the incorporation of clerks from the remaining Arms, the AGC consisted of over 7,500 officers and soldiers.

AGC Miscellaneous
In addition to the AGC personnel attached to major units throughout the Army the Corps is directly responsible for the following:

AGC Depot and Training Centre (Worthy Down)
Directorate Staff & Personnel Support (Worthy Down)
Directorate Educational & Training Services (Worthy Down)
Provost Marshal (Army) (Worthy Down)
Army Pay Office (Ashton)
Army Finance & Audit Office (Ashton)
Command Pay Offices (Hong Kong & Cyprus)
Regimental Pay Offices (Glasgow, Chester, Leicester, York, Exeter)
Defence Animal Centre (Melton Mobray)
RAVC Support Group (Aldershot)
Resettlement Centres (Catterick & York)

College of Military Education & Training Services (Beaconsfield)
Cadet Training Centre

Smaller Corps
THE INTELLIGENCE CORPS (Int Corps) - The Int Corps deals with operational intelligence, counter intelligence and security.

THE ROYAL ARMY VETERINARY CORPS (RAVC) - The RAVC look after the many animals that the Army has on strength. Veterinary tasks in today's army are mainly directed towards guard or search dogs and horses for ceremonial duties.

THE ARMY PHYSICAL TRAINING CORPS (APTC) - Consists mainly of SNCOs who are responsible for unit fitness. The majority of major units have a representative from this corps on their strength.

THE GENERAL SERVICE CORPS (GSC) - A holding unit for specialists. Personnel from this corps are generally members of the reserve army.

SMALL ARMS SCHOOL CORPS (SASC) - A small corps with the responsibility of training instructors in all aspects of weapon handling.

The Gibraltar Regiment
Consists of one infantry company and an artillery battery which assists in the defence of Gibraltar. We believe that there are plans to convert this regiment into an all infantry organisation for the defence of Gibraltar following the withdrawal of the last regular resident infantry battalion in 1991.

The Regular Army Reserve.

Every Officer or soldier completing a regular engagement has a liability for reserve service depending on the contract that he or she signed at the beginning of their regular engagement. A typical enlistment contract would state that regular service would be for a term of 9/22, meaning 9 years service with the colours and a remaining 13 years on the Regular Army Reserve to make up the 22 years of the contract. Officers remain on the reserve list until they are 55 years old.

On mobilisation the 195,300 men and women who are at present on the reserve list would be recalled for colour service, and in theory the size of the army would almost triple overnight. However, many of these reservists would have left the regular forces some time ago and it is generally acknowledged that a man who has been out of the service for five years or more would not be ready for front line duty. Equipment and procedures change fast and many reservists would require extensive retraining before being posted to active units.

An examination of the latest government figures show that about 110,000 men and women have left the Regular Army during the past 5 years and these reservists would probably be used to bring front line units up to war establishment.

The Territorial Army (TA) - Situation 1 September 1995

During late 1995 the TA consisted of approximately 59,000 personnel. On mobilisation, the TA would be expected to field a significant number of major units that would be used for the defence of the UK and the reinforcement of the ARRC in Germany. Many of these units have operational tasks that are just as demanding as those undertaken by regular soldiers and TA units earmarked for service in Germany have the same equipment as the regulars that they will support. A major effort is made to ensure that TA soldiers are trained to the highest standards.

TA soldiers are part-timers who devote much of their leisure to soldiering and although the standards in the TA vary from unit to unit, the overall standard is surprisingly high; with some units proving to be more than a match for their regular counterparts.

Each member of the TA has to complete 44 training days a year of which 15 days are spent at an annual camp or on a military base. For a full day's service TA soldiers are paid in line with regular rates of pay, and special payments are made for an evening's attendance at the local drill hall. All members of the TA receive an annual tax free cash payment known as "the bounty" which increases with each year of service.

Current plans appear to place a large part of the defence of the mainland UK in the hands of the TA. TA soldiers have been assigned national defence roles such as, guarding vital installations, undertaking reconnaissance and early warning,providing communications and damage control. In early 1995 a composite TA platoon served alongside the regular infantry component of the Falkland Islands garrison, and if this experiment is successful we believe that there will be a dramatic expansion of the scheme. TA Soldiers on short term contracts could prove to be valuable additions to regular units where manpower is at a premium.

TA Reorganisation

At the end of 1994 the UK MoD announced a wide ranging re-organisation of the TA that if anything appears to have enhanced its role and almost certainly ensures its long term survival. In general terms the TA will be formed in larger numbers of smaller units, and personnel will be part of either high readiness or ready reserve formations. The majority of the changes to the TA will be in place by 1 April 1996 and the broad outline of these changes is as follows:

Royal Armoured Corps

Will be organised into:
1 x Armoured Reconniassance Regiment
1 x NBC Defence Regiment
4 x National Defence Reconniassance Regiments
1 x Independent National Defence Reconnaissance Squadron
1 x Armoured Delivery Regiment

The Royal Yeomanry will re-role to form the NBC Defence Regiment equipped with Fuchs and Saxon armoured vehicles. The 8th Bn The Light Infantry will re-role as a National Defence Reconnaissance Regiment and the Queens Own Yeomanry will convert to the new Sabre CVR(T) vehicle. The armoured delivery regiment will form at the RAC Centre, Bovington to provide crews for replacement armoured vehicles and to deliver them to the front line.

Royal Artillery

2 x Field Regiments (FH-70)

3 x Air Defence Regiments (Javelin)
1 x Airmobile Battery (Light Gun)
1 x Commando Battery (Light Gun)
1 x Airborne Battery (Light Gun)
Honourable Artillery Company

Royal Engineers
5 x General Support Regiments
3 x Air Support Regiments
1 x Explosive Ordnance Disposal Regiment
1 x Commando Squadron
1 x Topographic Squadron
1 x Independent Field Park Squadron
1 x Field Park Squadron
Civil Affairs Organisation
Military Works Force

Royal Signals
3 x Ptarmigan Regiments
2 x Euromux Regiments
6 x National Communications Regiments
3 x Independent Signals Squadrons
2 x Special Communications Squadrons

Two (National Communications) Brigade units will be restructured to provide Regional and National Communications support to Land Command. An independent Combat Service Support Group Squadron will also be formed.

Infantry
In the future all TA Infantry Battalions, including Parachute Battalions, will have a common establishment of three Rifle Companies and a Headquarters Company. In addition there will be 4 x Fire Support Battalions with mortar, Milan and machine gun platoons. Following re-organisation there will be:

29 x General Reserve TA Battalions
4 x Fire Support Battalions

Army Air Corps
1 x Aviation Regiment

Royal Logistic Corps
1 x HQ Transport Group
1 x HQ Postal and Courier Group
8 x Transport Regiments
2 x Ambulance Regiments
3 x Postal and Courier Regiments
1 x Supply Regiment
1 x Pioneer Regiment
1 x Port Regiment
2 x Movement Control Regiments
1 x Catering Support Regiment
1 x Training Regiment
19 x Specialist Squadrons

Army Medical Services
11 x Field Hospitals
7 x Field Ambulances
1 x Parachute Medical Squadron
1 x Ambulance Train Group
13 x Specialist Medical Teams
1 x Field Medical Equipment Depot

Field Hospitals will now be restructured to consist of a Headquarters with 2 Surgical Teams with 100 beds and 2 x sub-units each with 1 x Surgical Team and 50 beds.

Royal Electrical & Mechanical Engineers
5 x Equipment Support Battalions

Current TA Major Units

However during late 1995 the following is a reasonable reflection of the TA Major Unit situation:

Cavalry

The Royal Yeomanry	RY
The Queen's Own Yeomanry	QOY
The Royal Wessex Yeomanry	R WX Y
The Royal Mercian & Lancastrian Yeomanry	R ML Y
The Scottish Yeomanry	SCOT Y

Artillery

Honourable Artillery Company	102 AD Regt
100 Fd Regt	103 AD Regt
101 Fd Regt	104 AD Regt

Infantry

Scottish Division

1/52 Lowland
2/52 Lowland
1/51 Highland
2/51 Highland
3/51 Highland

Kings Division

4 King's Own Border
5/8 King's
4 QLR
4/5 Green Howards
3 PWO
3 DWR

Light Division

5 LI
6 LI
7 LI
8 LI
4 RGJ
5 RGJ
21 SAS & 23 SAS

Queens Division

5 PWRR	5 R Anglian
6/7 PWRR	6 R Anglian
Londons	7 R Anglian
5 RRF	
6 RRF	

Prince of Wales's Division

1 Wessex	3 WFR
2 Wessex	3 Staffords
4 D & D	
3 Cheshire	
3 RWF	
3/4 RRW	

Parachute Regiment

4 Para
10 Para

The Royal Irish Regiment

4/5 Rangers

Engineers

R MON RE (M)	75 Engr Regt
71 Engr Regt	76 Engr Regt
72 Engr Regt	77 Engr Regt
73 Engr Regt	78 Engr Regt
74 Engr Regt	101 Engr Regt (EOD)
	111 Engr Regt

Note: The above list is not in order of precedence

Major Army Equipment

Fv 4030/4 Challenger 1
(Approx 350 in Operational Service on 1 Jan 1996 - being replaced by Challenger 2 from mid 1995). Armament 1 x 120mm L11A7 gun: 2 x 7.62 Machine Guns: 2 x 5 barrel smoke dischargers: Engine Rolls-Royce CV12: Ammunition Capacity 44 rounds of 120mm: 6000 rounds of 7.62mm: Engine Power 1,200 bhp at 2,300 rpm: Engine Capacity 26.1 litres: Max Road Speed 56kph: Weight loaded 62,000kg: Length Hull 9.87m: Length Gun Forward 11.55m: Height 3.04m: Width 3.42m: Ground Clearance O.5m: Crew 4: Ground Pressure 0.96 kg/cm2: Fording Depth (no prep) 1.07m.

Produced by the Royal Ordnance Factory in Leeds the first Challengers 1 were delivered to the British Army in 1983.

Challenger 1 is a development of the Centurion/Chieftain line which was modified to produce the Shir/Iran 2 originally planned for service with the Iranian forces. After the Iranian Revolution the Shir Iran 2 project was taken over by the British Army and the end result was Challenger later re-designated as Challenger 1.

The main differences between Challenger 1 and its predecessor Chieftain (the

MBT that it replaced) were in the engine and armour. The Challenger engine, which produces 1,200bhp at 2,300rpm was far more powerful than the Chieftain engine, and the Chobham Armour carried is believed to give protection from almost all types of anti-tank weapon. Chobham armour is thought to consist of several layers of nylon micromesh, bonded on both sides by sheets of titanium alloy, in addition to several other layers of specialised armour and ceramics. Challenger 1 is believed to have cost about £2 million per vehicle at 1990 prices.

The main armament on all Challenger 1's is currently being upgraded by the installation of the L30 CHARM gun. In addition to firing the existing range of ammunition, this gun fires a new armour piercing fin stabilised discarding sabot round with a depleted uranium warhead, which should be able to defeat the armour on all known MBT's. An additional improvement is the ACTAS (Active Cupola Target Acquisition System) which has been retrofitted to all Challenger 1's. This system permits the use of the commanders cupola for target acquisition and designation to the gunner.

The only nation known to be operating Challenger 1 other than the UK is Jordan, where the 274 tanks in service are known as Khalid. The UK also operates approximately 77 Challenger 1 ARV's and 16 Challenger 1 driver training tanks.

Challenger 2

(386 Challenger 2 on Order) Crew 4; Length Gun Forward 11.55m; Hull Length 8.32m; Height to Turret Roof 2.49m; Width 3.52m; Ground Clearance 0.50m; Combat Weight 62,500 kgs; Main Armament 1 x 120mm L30 CHARM Gun; Ammunition Carried 52 rounds - APFSDS, HESH, Smoke, DU; Secondary Armament Co-axial 7.62mm MG; 7.62mm GPMG Turret Mounted for Air Defence; Ammunition Carried 4000 rounds 7.62mm; Engine CV12TCA 12 cylinder - Auxiliary Engine Perkins 4.108 4 - stroke diesel; Gearbox TN54 epicyclic - 6 forward gears and 2 reverse; Road Speed 56 kph; Cross Country Speed 40 kph; Fuel Capacity 1,797 litres.

In July 1991 the UK MOD announced an order for 127 x Challenger 2 MBT and 13 driver training tanks. This initial order was followed in July 1994 by a further contract for 259 vehicles to make a total of 386. This will be enough to equip 8 regiments with the vehicle and allow 82 tanks for training and reserve. A regiment will have 38 tanks in three squadrons. Challenger 2 is manufactured by Vickers Defence Systems and production will be undertaken at their factories in Newcastle-Upon-Tyne and Leeds. At 1995 prices Challenger 2 is believed to cost £2.5 million per vehicle.

Although the hull and automotive parts of the Challenger 2 are based upon that of its predecessor Challenger 1, the new tank incorporates over 150 improvements aimed at increasing reliability and maintainability. The whole of the Challenger 2 turret is of a totally new design and the vehicle has a crew of four - commander, gunner, loader/signaller and driver. The 120mm rifled Royal Ordnance L30 gun fires all current tank ammunition plus the new depleted uranium (DU) round with a stick charge propellant system.

The design of the turret incorporates several of the significant features that Vickers had developed for its Mk 7 MBT (a Vickers turret on a Leopard 2 chassis). The central feature is an entirely new fire control system based on the Ballistic Control System developed by Computing Devices Company (Canada) for the US Army's M1A1 MBT. This second generation computer incorporates dual 32-bit processors with a MIL STD1553B databus and has sufficient growth potential to accept Battlefield Information Control System (BICS) functions and navigation aids (a GPS satnav system). The armour is an uprated version of Challenger 1's Chobham armour.

The first production models of the Challenger 2 were taken into service by the Royal Scots Dragoon Guards in mid 1994 and the regiment was the first to deploy to Germany with the new tank in mid 1995. The actual in service date (ISD) for the vehicle is December 1995 and we would expect to see all 386 Challenger 2's in service with the British Army by the end of the decade.

The only export order so far is an Omani order for 18 x Challenger 2 MBTs, 2 x Driver Training Vehicles and 4 x Challenger Armoured Repair and Recovery

Vehicles signed during 1993. However, Vickers Defence Systems have high hopes for the vehicle in the remainder of the world market during the next ten years.

MCV - 80 Fv 510 (Warrior)

(789 In Service) Weight loaded 24,500kg: Length 6.34m: Height to turret top 2.78m: Width 3.0m: Ground Clearance 0.5m: Max Road Speed 75kph: Road Range 500km: Engine Rolls Royce CV8 diesel: Horsepower 550hp: Crew 2 (carries 8 infantry soldiers): Armament L21 30mm Rarden Cannon: Coaxial EX-34 7.62mm Chain Gun: Smoke Dischargers Royal Ordnance Visual and Infra Red Screening Smoke (VIRSS).

Warrior is an armoured infantry fighting vehicle (AIFV) that replaced the AFV 432 in the armoured infantry battalions. Following drawdown the original buy of 1,048 vehicles was reduced and in early 1993 it was announced that the total buy had been reduced to 789 units. The vehicle is in service with 2 armoured infantry battalions in the UK (with 3 (UK) Div) and 6 armoured infantry battalions in Germany (with 1 (UK) Armd Div). Warrior armed with the 30mmm Rarden cannon gives the crew a good chance of destroying enemy APC's at ranges of up to 1,500m and the vehicle carries an infantry section of eight men.

The vehicle is NBC proof, and a full range of night vision equipment is included as standard. The basic Warrior is part of a family of vehicles which include a milan carrier, a mechanised recovery vehicle, an engineer combat version and an artillery command vehicle to name but a few. Examination of the contract details reveal that each vehicle will cost approximately £550,000 pounds.

The vehicle has seen successful operational service in the Gulf (1991) and with the British contingent serving with the UN in Bosnia. The vehicle has proven protection against mines, and there is dramatic BBC TV footage of a Warrior running over a Serbian anti tank mine with little or no serious damage to the vehicle.

The Kuwait MoD has signed a contract for the purchase of warrior vehicles some of which are Recce vehicles armed with a 90mm Cockerill gun. Industry sources suggest that the Kuwait contract is for 230 vehicles.

AT - 105 Saxon
(664 in service) Weight 10,670kg: Length 5.16m: Width 2.48m: Height 2.63m: Ground Clearance (axles) 0.33m: Max Road Speed 96kph: Max Road Range 510km: Fuel Capacity 160 litres: Fording 1.12m: Gradient 60 degrees: Engine Bedford 600 6-cylinder diesel developing 164bhp at 2,800rpm: Armour proof against 7.62 rounds fired at point blank range: Crew 2 + 10 max.

The Saxon is manufactured by GKN Defence and the first of the 664 units for the British Army were delivered in late 1983. The vehicle, which can be best described as a battlefield taxi is designed around truck parts and does not require the enormous maintenance of track and running gear normally associated with APC/AIFVs. Capable of travelling across very rough terrain and fording over 3' of water, the Saxon is a welcome addition to the inventory of infantry units in UKLF providing much needed battlefield mobility. The vehicle is fitted with a 7.62mm Machine Gun for LLAD.

Each vehicle costs over £100,000 at 1984 prices and they are on issue to 4 mechanised infantry assigned to 3 (UK) Division infantry battalions. The vehicle has been used very sucessfully by British mechanised battalions serving with the UN in Bosnia where the addition of an L37 turret has enhanced its firepower.
During 1993 the British Army took delivery of the Saxon patrol vehicle for service in Northern Ireland. This new vehicle has a Cummins BT 5.1 engine instead of the Beford 6 cyclinder installed on the APC version and other enhancements for internal security operations such as roof mounted searchlights, improved armour, a barricade removal device and an anti-wire device.

Saxon Patrol comes in two versions, troop carrier and ambulance. The troop carrier carries ten men and the ambulance 2 stretcher cases. Industry sources suggest that this latest contract was for 137 vehicles at a cost of some 20 million resulting in a unit cost per vehicle of approximately £145,000.

Milan 2

Missile - Max Range 2,000m; Mix Range 25m; Length 918mm; Weight 6.73Kg; Diameter 125mm; Wing Span 267mm; Rate of Fire 3-4rpm; Warhead - Weight 2.70kg; Diameter 115mm; Explosive Content 1.79kg; Firing Post- Weight 16.4kg; Length 900mm; Height 650mm; Width 420mm; Armour Penetration 352mm; Time of Flight to Max Range 12.5 secs; Missile Speed 720kph; Guidance Semi-Automatic command to line of sight by means of wires:

Milan is a second generation anti-tank weapon, the result of a joint development project between France and West Germany with British Milan launchers and missiles built under licence in the UK by British Aerospace Dynamics. We believe that the cost of a Milan missile is currently in the region of £9,000 and that to date the UK MOD has purchased over 50,000 missiles. The Milan comes in two main components which are the launcher and the missile, it then being a simple matter to clip both items together and prepare the system for use. On firing the operator has only to keep his aiming mark on the target and the SACLOS guidance system will do the rest.

Milan was the first of a series of infantry anti-tank weapons that seriously started to challenge the supremacy of the main battle tank on the battlefield.
During fighting in Chad in 1987 it appears that 12 Chadian Milan posts mounted on Toyota Light Trucks were able to account for over 60 Libyan T-55's and T-62's. Reports from other conflicts suggest similar results.

Milan is on issue throughout the British Army and an armoured infantry battalion could be expected to be equipped with 24 firing posts and 200 missiles. In the longer term we expect to see Milan replaced by Trigat MR in the latter part of the decade. Milan is in service with 36 nations world-wide and it is believed that there are over 1,000 firing posts in service with the British Army.

Trigat MR
Range 2000m: Missile Weight 16kg: Firing Post Weight 20kg.

Trigat MR (Medium Range) is a manportable or vehicle borne, third generation anti-tank missile system designed to replace Milan in service with the British Army. Trigat MR is a medium range missile (2000m) with SACLOS beam riding guidance. Launch will be low velocity, with thrust vectoring keeping the missile airborne as the aerodynamic surfaces come into effect.

The missile is the result of a European collaborative project with the three main partners being France, Germany and the UK. The manufacturer is Euromissile Dynamics Group (EDMG). Current predictions are that the missiles may cost as much as £25,000 each by the time that the system is accepted into service. We believe that Trigat MR should appear in service during December 1998.

5.56mm Individual Weapon (IW) (SA 80)
Effective Range 400m: Muzzle Velocity 940m/s: Rate of Fire from 610-775rpm: Weight 4.98kg (with 30 round magazine): Length Overall 785mm: Barrel Length 518mm: Trigger Pull 3.12-4.5kg.

Designed to fire the standard NATO 5.56mm x 45mm round the SA 80 is fitted with an X4 telescopic (SUSAT) sight as standard. Although some modification work is still in progress, the vast majority of the British Army is now equipped with this weapon. The total buy for SA 80 is for 332,092 weapons.
Issues of the weapon are believed to be as follows: Royal Navy 7,864; Royal Marines 8,350; Royal Air Force 42,221; MOD Police 1,878; Army 271,779.

At 1991/92 prices the total cost of the SA80 Contract was in the order of £384.16 million. By late 1994 some 10,000 SA 80 Night Sights and 3rd Generation Image Intensifier Tubes had been delivered almost completing the contract.

The weapon has had a mixed press and much has been made of the 32 modifications that have been made to the SA80 since 1983. Although there are many critics outside of the services, in the main the serving soldiers that we have spoken to have praised the weapon, and those that have had experience on both the SLR and SA80 are unstinting in their praise for the newer system.

AS 90

(179 on order) Crew 5: Length 9.07m: Width 3.3m: Height 3.0m overall: Ground Clearance 0.41m: Turret Ring Diameter 2.7m: Armour 17mm: Calibre 155mm: Range (39 cal) 24.7kms (52 cal) 30kms: Recoil Length 780mm: Rate of Fire 3 rounds in 10 secs (burst) 6 rounds per minute (intense) 2 rounds per minute (sustained): Secondary Armament 7.62mm MG: Traverse 6,400 mills: Elevation -89/+1.244 mills: Ammunition Carried 48 x 155mm projectiles and charges (31 turret & 17 hull): Engine Cummins VTA903T turbo-charged V8 diesel 660hp: Max Speed 53 kph: Gradient 60%: Vertical Obstacle 0.75m: Trench Crossing 2.8m: Fording Depth 1.5m: Road Range 420kms.

AS 90 is manufactured by Vickers Shipbuilding and Engineering (VSEL) at Barrow in Furness and in 1992 was the subject of an order for 179 guns under a fixed price contract for £300 million. These 179 guns are equipping 5 field regiments, completely replacing the Abbot and M109 in British service. The first Regiment to receive AS 90 was 1st Regiment Royal Horse Artillery (1 RHA) in October 1993, followed by issues to 3 RHA, 4 Regt, 40 Regt and 26 Regt. Each Regiment will receive 4 batterys of eight guns, of which six will be manned in peacetime. Three of these Regiments will be under the command of 1(UK) Armoured Division in Germany and two under the command of 3 (UK) Div in the United Kingdom. Production of AS 90 should be complete by late 1995.

AS 90 is currently equipped with a 39 calibre gun which fires the NATO L15 unassisted projectile out to a range of 24.7kms (RAP range is 30kms). It is believed that future production models may have the 52 calibre gun with ranges of 30kms (unassisted) and 40kms (assisted projectile). Indications are that the current in service date for the 52 calibre gun is 1998.

AS 90 has been fitted with an autonomous navigation and gun laying system (AGLS), enabling it to work independently of external sighting references.
Central to the system is is an inertial dynamic reference unit (DRU) taken from the US Army's MAPS (Modular Azimuth Positioning System). The bulk of the turret electronics are housed in the Turret Control Computer (TCC) which controls the main turret functions, including gunlaying, magazine control, loading systems control, power distribution and testing.

227mm MLRS

(62 launchers in service - 54 operational in 3 Regiments): Crew 3: Weight loaded 24,756kg: Weight Unloaded 19,573kg: Length 7.167m: Width 2.97m: Height (stowed) 2.57m: Height (max elevatation) 5.92m: Ground Clearance 0.43m: Max Road Speed 64kph: Road Range 480km: Fuel Capacity 617 litres: Fording 1.02m: Vertical Obstacle 0.76m: Engine Cummings VTA-903 turbo-charged 8 cylinder diesel developing 500 bhp at 2,300 rpm: Rocket Diameter 227mm: Rocket Length 3.93m: M77 Bomblet Rocket Weight 302.5kg: AT2 SCATMIN Rocket Weight 254.46kg: M77 Bomblet Range 11.5 -32kms: AT2 SCATMIN Rocket Range 39kms: One round "Fire for Effect" equals one launcher firing 12 rockets: Ammuniton Carried 12 rounds (ready to fire).

The British Army has purchased MLRS to replace the M107 SP Guns that were previously deployed with Corps Artillery Heavy Regiments. The MLRS is based on the US M2 Bradley chassis and the system is self loaded with 2 x rocket pod containers, each containing 6 x rockets. The whole loading sequence is power assisted and loading takes between 20 and 40 minutes. There is no manual proceedure.

A single round "Fire for Effect" (12 rockets) delivers 7728 bomblets or 336 scatterable mines and the coverage achieved is considered sufficient to neutalise a 500m x 500m target or produce a minefield of a similar size. The weapon system is range dependent and therefore more rounds will be required to guarantee the effect as the range to the target increases. Ammunition for the MLRS is carried on the DROPS vehicle which is a Medium Mobility Load Carrier. Each DROPS vehicle with a trailer can carry 8 x Rocket Pod Containers and there are 15 x DROPS vehicles supporting the 9 x M270 Launcher vehicles within each MLRS battery.

The handling of MLRS is almost a military "art form" and is an excellent example of the dependence of modern artillery on high technology. Getting the best out of the system is more than just parking the tubes and firing in the direction of the enemy. MLRS is the final link in a chain that includes almost everything available on the modern battlefield, from high speed commnications, collation of intelligence, logistics and a multitude of high technology artillery skills and drills. Remotely piloted vehicles can be used to acquire targets, real time TV and data links are used to move information from target areas to formation commanders and onward to the firing positions. Helicopters can be used to dump ammunition and in some cases to move firing platforms.

MLRS will probably be deployed as independent launcher units, using "shoot-and-scoot" techniques. A battery of nine launchers will be given a battery manoeuvre area (BMA), within which are allocated three troop manoeuvre areas (TMA). These TMAs will contain close hides, survey points and reload points. In a typical engagement, a single launcher will be given its fire mission orders using burst data transmission.

An important initial piece of information received is the "drive on angle"; the crew will drive the launcher out of the hide (usually less than 100m) and align it with this angle. Using the navigation equipment, its location is fed into the ballistic computer which already has the full fire mission details. The launcher is then elevated and fired and the process can take as little as a few minutes to complete.

As soon as conditions allow, the vehicle will leave the firing location and go to a reload point where it will unload the empty rocket pods and pick up a full one; this can be done in less than five minutes. It will then go to a new hide within the TMA via a survey point to check the accuracy of the navigation system (upon which the accuracy of fire is entirely dependent). The whole of this cycle is coordinated centrally and details of the new hide and reload point are received as part of the fire mssion orders. The complete cycle from firing to being in new hide ready for action might take half an hour.

In a typical day, a battery could move once or twice to a new BMA but this could impose a strain upon the re-supply system unless well planned (bearing in mind the need for the ammunition to be in position before the launcher vehicle arrives in a new BMA).

The frequent moves are a result of security problems inherent in MLRS's use. In addition to attack by radar-controlled counter battery fire, its effectiveness as an interdiction weapon makes it a valuable target for special-forces units. Although MLRS will be hidden amongst friendly forces up to 15km behind the FEBA, its firing signature and small crew (three) will force it to move continually to avoid an actual confrontation with enemy troops.

The US Army is currently operating 416 MLRS and by the middle of the decade the French will have 82, the West Germans 206 and the Italians 21.

Starstreak
(135 Fire Units on Order) Missile Length 1.39m: Missile Diameter 0.27m: Missile Speed Mach 4+: Maximum Range 7 kms: Minimum Range 300m.

Short Brothers of Belfast are the prime contractors for the Starstreak HVM (Hyper Velocity Missile) which continues along the development path of both Blowpipe and Javelin. The system can be shoulder launched using the LML (lightweight multiple launcher) or vehicle borne on the Alvis Stormer APC. The Stormer APC has an eight round launcher and 12 reload missiles can be carried inside the vehicle. Starstreak which has been designed to counter threats from very high performance low flying aircraft and fast pop-up type strikes by attack helicopters, can easily be retrofitted to existing Blowpipe and Javelin equipment. The missile employs a system of three dart type projectiles which can make multiple hits on the target. Each of these darts has an explosive warhead combined with a chemical and kinetic energy penetrating shell. It is believed that the Starstreak has an SSK (single shot to kill) probability of over 95%.

During 1994, 47 Regiment stationed at Thorney Island in the UK was issued with HVM mounted on Stormer.

Rapier
(120 fire units in service). Guidance Semi Automatic to line of Sight (SACLOS): Missile Diameter 13.3 cm: Missile Length 2.35m: Rocket Solid Fuelled: Warhead High Explosive: Launch Weight 42kg: Speed Mach 2+: Ceiling 3,000m: Maximum Range 6,800m: Fire Unit Height 2.13m: Fire Unit Weight 1,227kg: Radar Height (in action) 3.37m: Radar Weight 1,186kg: Optical Tracker Height 1.54m: Optical Tracker Weight 119kg: Generator Weight 243kg: Generator Height 0.91m.

The Rapier system provides area, Low Level Air Defence (LLAD) over the battlefield. It consists of an Optical Tracker, a Fire Unit, a Radar and a Generator. The into-action time of the system is thought to be about 15 minutes and the radar is believed to scan out to 12km. Each fire unit can therefore cover an Air Defence Area (ADA) of about 100 square kms. Having discharged the 4 missiles on a Fire Unit, 2 men are thought to be able to carry out a reload in about 3 minutes.

The Royal Artillery has 2 regiments equipped with Rapier, 1 in Germany with the ARRC and one in UKLF. Each regiment has 3/4 batterys and each battery 10 fire units. In the Falklands Campaign, Rapier was credited with 14 kills and 6 probables from a total of 24 missiles fired.

We believe that three of the seven Rapier Batterys in service with the British Army have been upgraded to Field Standard B2 (with Darkfire Electro optical tracker and new surveillance radars).

In the longer term there will be a further upgrade to Field Standard C (known as Rapier 2000) and that three batterys (31 fire units) of this equipment are currently on order. The towed system launcher will mount eight missiles (able to fire two simultaneously) which will be manufactured in two warhead versions. One of these warheads will be armour piercing to deal with fixed wing targets, and the other a fragmentation warhead for the engagement of cruise missiles and RPVs. Rapier 2000 will have the Darkfire tracker and a tailor made 3-dimensional radar system for target acquisition developed by Plessey. The total cost of the Rapier FS"C" programme is £1,886 million.

Rapier has now been sold to the armed forces of at least 14 nations. We believe that sales have amounted to over 25,000 missiles, 600 launchers and 350 Blindfire radars.

There are 40 Tracked Rapier units available mounted on the US M548 chasis.

Lynx AH - Mark 1/7/9

(126 in service). Length Fuselage 12.06m: Height 3.4m: Rotor Diameter 12.8m: Max Speed 330kph: Cruising Speed 232kph: Range 885km: Engines 2 Rolls-Royce Gem 41: Power 2 x 850 bhp: Fuel Capacity 918 litres(internal): Weight (max take off) 4,763kg: Crew one pilot, one air-gunner/observer: Armament 8 x TOW Anti-Tank Missiles: -4 7.62mm machine guns: Passengers-able to carry 10 PAX: Combat radius approx 100kms with 2 hour loiter.

Lynx is the helicopter used by the British Army to counter the threat posed by enemy armoured formations. Armed with 8 x TOW missiles the Lynx is now the mainstay of the British armed helicopter fleet. However, in addition to its role as an anti-tank helicopter, Lynx can be used for fire support using machine guns, troop lifts, casualty evacuation and many more vital battlefield tasks.

During hostilities we would expect Lynx to operate on a section basis, with 2 or 3 Lynx aircraft armed with TOW directed by a Section Commander possibly flying in a Gazelle. The Section Commander would control what is in reality an airborne tank ambush and following an attack on enemy armour decide when to break contact. Having broken contact, the aircraft would return to a forward base to refuel and rearm. Working from forward bases, some of which are within 10kms of the FEBA, it is suggested that a Lynx section could be "turned around" in less than 15 minutes. Lynx with the TOW ATGW (range 3,750m) replaced SCOUT with SS11 as the British Army's anti-tank helicopter.

We believe the majority of Lynx in British service to be Lynx Mark 7 and that there are currently 24 Lynx Mark 9 (the latest version) in the inventory.
Lynx is known to be in service with France, Brazil, Argentina, The Netherlands, Qatar, Denmark, Norway, West Germany and Nigeria. The naval version carries anti-ship missiles.

Longbow Apache

(67 On Order) Gross Mission Weight 7,746 kgs (17,077 lb; Cruise Speed at 500 meters 272 kph; Maximum Range (Internal Fuel with 20 minute reserve) 462 kms; General Service Ceiling 3,505 meters (11,500 ft); Crew 2; Carries - 16 x Hellfire II missiles (range 6,000 meters approx); 76 x 2.75" rockets; 1,200 30mm cannon rounds; 4 x Air to Air Missiles; Engines 2 x Rolls Royce RTM-332.

The UK MoD ordered 67 Longbow Apache from Westland during mid 1995 with an ISD towards the end of the decade. From this figure of 67 aircraft we believe that there will be 48 aircraft in two regiments (each of 24 aircraft). The remaining 19 aircraft will be used for trials, training and a war maintenance reserve (WMR).

The procurement of an attack helicopter of this type gives the British Army the "punch" necessary for operations during the next decade. These aircraft had a significant effect upon operations during the 1991 Gulf War where the US Army deployed 288 x AH-64 Apache in 15 Army Aviation battalions. The US Army claim that these aircraft destroyed 120 x APCs, 500 x MBT, 120 x Artillery Guns, 10 Radar Installations, 10 x Helicopters, 30 x Air Defence Units, about 300 soft skinned vehicles and 10 x fixed wing aircraft on the ground. A single Army Aviation AH-64 battalion is believed to have destroyed 40 x APCs and over 100 x MBT in an engagement that lasted over 3 hours, firing 107 Hellfire missiles and over 300 x 70mm rockets.

BR90 Family of Bridges

In early 1994 the UK MOD announced that the production order had been placed for the BR90 family of bridges that are planned to enter service between January 1996 and June 1997 as follows:

January 1996	-	General Support Bridge
November 1996	-	Close Support Bridge
May 1997	-	Two Span Bridge
June 1997	-	Long Span Bridge

BR90 will be deployed with Royal Engineer units in both Germany and the United Kingdom. The production order was issued and accepted in October 1993 and the value of the order is approximately £140 million. This order will secure up to 250 jobs at the prime contractor, Thompson Defence Projects in Wolverhampton, as well as 50 jobs at Unipower in Watford plus many other sub-contractors.

The components of the system are:

Close Support Bridge - This consists of three tank launched bridges capable of being carried on the in-service Chieftain bridgelayer and a TBT (Tank Bridge Transporter) truck.

	Weight	Length	Gap
No 10 Bridge	13 tons	26m	24.5m
No 11 Bridge	7.4 tons	16m	14.5m
No 12 Bridge	5.3 tons	13.5m	12m

The existing No 8 and No 9 bridges carried in the Chieftain AVLB will be retained in service.

The Unipower TBT 8 x 8 truck can carry 1 x No 1 Bridge, 1 x No 11 Bridge or 2 x No 12 Bridges. The TBT has an unladen weight of 21 tons and is also used to transport the General Support Bridge.

General Support Bridge - This system utilises the Automotive Bridge Launching Equipment (ABLE) that is capable of launching bridges up to 44 metres in length. The ABLE vehicle is positioned with its rear pointing across the gap to be crossed and a lightweight launch rail extended across the gap.

The bridge is then assembled and winched across the gap supported by the rail, with sections added until the gap is crossed. Once the bridge has crossed the gap the ABLE launch rail is recovered. A standard ABLE system set consists of an ABLE vehicle and 2 x TBT carrying a 32 metre bridge set.

It is believed that a 32m bridge can be built by 10 men in about 25 minutes.

Spanning Systems - There are two basic spanning systems. The long span systems allows for lengthening a 32 metre span to 44 metres using ABLE and the two span system allows 2 x 32 metre bridge sets to be constructed by ABLE and secured in the middle by piers or floating pontoons, crossing a total gap of about 60 metres.

PART 4 - THE ROYAL AIR FORCE
Royal Air Force Squadrons (as at 1 January 1996)

	1996	1980
Strike/Attack Squadrons	6	14
Offensive Support Squadrons	5	5
Air Defence Squadrons	6	16
Maritime Patrol Squadrons	3	4
Reconnaissance Squadrons	5	5
Airborne Early Warning Squadrons	1	1
Transport/Tanker Squadrons	8	9
Helicopter Squadrons	9	4
Tanker Squadrons	1	2
Search & Rescue Squadrons	2	2
Surface to Air Missile Squadrons	5	8
Ground Defence Squadrons	5	5
TOTAL SQUADRONS	51	71

Note: 1980 Figures are for comparison purposes. The total RAF Manpower figures for 1 April 1995 are as follows:

Officers	12,800	(1,000)
Other Ranks	57,900	(300)
	70,700	(1,300)

Figures in brackets relate to personel undergoing basic training. Planned redundancies will bring this manpower figure down to 52,500 "by the end of the century". In December 1994 8,600 RAF redundancies were announced, 3,000 for late 1995 and a further 5,600 during 1996

Royal Air Force Squadron Listing (as at 1 January 1996)

1 Sqn	13 x Harrier	RAF Wittering
2 Sqn	12 x Tornado GR1A (1)	RAF Marham
3 Sqn	13 x Harrier	RAF Laarbruch(closure 99)
4 Sqn	13 x Harrier	RAF Laarbruch(closure 99)

5 Sqn	12 x Tornado F3 (1)	RAF Coningsby
6 Sqn	12 x Jaguar GR1A (1)	RAF Coltishall
	1 x Jaguar T2A	
7 Sqn	9 x Chinook HC3 (3)	RAF Odiham
	1 x Gazelle HT3	
8 Sqn	6 x E-3D Sentry (1)	RAF Waddington
9 Sqn	12 x Tornado GR1 (1)	RAF Bruggen
10 Sqn	8 x VC10 C1/C1K (2)	RAF Brize Norton
11 Sqn	15 x Tornado F3 (1)	RAF Leeming
12 Sqn	12 x Tornado GR1B (1)	RAF Lossiemouth
13 Sqn	12 x Tornado GR1A (1)	RAF Marham
14 Sqn	12 x Tornado GR1 (1)	RAF Bruggen
17 Sqn	12 x Tornado GR1 (1)	RAF Bruggen
18 Sqn	3 x Chinook HC2 (1)	RAF Laarbruch (closure 99)
	4 x Puma HC1 (1)	
19(R)Sqn	13 x Hawk	RAF Valley
22 Sqn	5 x Sea King HAR3 (1)	Wattisham
	2 x Wessex HC2 (2)	RAF Valley
24 Sqn	12 x Hercules C1/C3/C1K (1)	RAF Lyneham
25 Sqn	15 x Tornado F3 (1)	RAF Leeming
28 Sqn	4 x Wessex HC2 (2)	RAF Sek Kong
29 Sqn	12 x Tornado F3 (1)	RAF Coningsby
30 Sqn	12 x Hercules C1/C3/C1K (1)	RAF Lyneham
31 Sqn	12 x Tornado GR1 (1)	RAF Bruggen
32 (Royal) Sqn	7 x BAe 125 (1)	RAF Northolt
	3 x BAe 146	
	4 x Wessex HCC4	
33 Sqn	10 x Puma (2)	RAF Odiham
39 Sqn	(1 PRU) 5 x Canberra (4)	RAF Marham
41 Sqn	12 x Jaguar GR1A (1)	RAF Coltishall
	1 x Jaguar T2A	
42 (R) Sqn	3 x Nimrod MR2	RAF Kinloss
43 Sqn	13 x Tornado F3 (1)	RAF Leuchars
47 Sqn	12 x Hercules C1/C3 (1)	RAF Lyneham
51 Sqn	3 x Nimrod R1	RAF Waddington
54 Sqn	12 x Jaguar GR1A (2)	RAF Coltishall

60 Sqn	8 x Wessex HC2	RAF Benson
70 Sqn	11 x Hercules C1/C3 (2)	RAF Lyneham
72 Sqn	13 x Wessex HC2 (2)	RAF Aldergrove
78 Sqn	1 x Chinook HC2 (1)	RAF Mount Pleasant
84 Sqn	3 x Wessex HC2 (2)	RAF Akrotiri
101 Sqn	13 x VC10 K2/K3/K4 (1)	RAF Brize Norton
100 Sqn	13 x Hawk T1/T1A (1)	RAF Leeming
111 Sqn	13 x Tornado F3 (1)	RAF Leuchars
120 Sqn	7 x Nimrod MR2 (1)	RAF Kinloss
201 Sqn	7 x Nimrod MR2 (1)	RAF Kinloss
202 Sqn	7 x Sea King HAR3 (2)	RAF Lossiemouth (*)
206 Sqn	7 x Nimrod MR2	RAF Kinloss
216 Sqn	8 x Tristar K1/KC1/C2 (2)	RAF Brize Norton
230 Sqn	13 x Puma HC1 (2)	RAF Aldergrove
617 Sqn	12 x Tornado GR1B (1)	RAF Lossiemouth
1312 Flight	2 x Hercules C1K	RAF Mount Pleasant

Notes:

* 202 Sqn has detachments at RAF Boulmer and Leconfield

(1) The figures for aircraft in squadrons are the Aircraft Establishment (AE) figures and represent the numbers of aircraft that are manned and fully resourced. The figure in brackets directly following the aircraft type are the In Use Reserve (IUR) figures and show the numbers of aircraft held to enable the AE aircraft to undergo servicing, Modifications or repair.

(2) There are RAF flying units deployed in the Arabian Gulf (Op Jural) and Turkey (Op Warden) in support of United Nations operations in the Iraq no-fly zones.

(3) In addition, RAF units are supporting UN Operations in the area of the former Yugoslavia - Operation Deny Flight, with transport units supplying essential items to areas such as Sarajevo, and fast jets operating from the airbase at Gioia de Colle in Italy to police the "no flying zone".

(4) RAF Stations at Finningley and Scampton are to close in mid 1996 with the Red Arrows relocating to RAF Cranwell. RAF Laarbruch will close in 1999 and the Harrier force will almost certainly re-locate to the UK

Training Units

15 (R) Sqn	16 x TornadoGR1	RAF Lossiemouth
16 (R) Sqn	4 x Jaguar T2A	RAF Lossiemouth
	4 x Jaguar GR1A	
20 (R) Sqn	9 x Harrier GR7	RAF Wittering
	6 x Harrier T10	
27 (R) Sqn	5 x Chinook HC2	RAF Odiham
	4 x Puma	
42 (R) Sqn	3 x Nimrod MR2	RAF Kinloss
56 (R) Sqn	20 x Tornado F3	RAF Coningsby
57 (R) Sqn	5 x Hercules C1/C3	RAF Lyneham
Sea King Training Unit	3 x Sea King HAR3	RAF St Mawgan
SAR Training Unit	4 x Wessex HC2	RAF Valley
Tri National Training Unit	14 x Tornado GR1	RAF Cottesmore
RAF Aerobatic Team	10 x Hawk T1/T1A	RAF Cranwell

Note: The (R) in a squadron designation represents a training unit/reserve squadron. In the majority of cases this reserve squadron is the Operational Conversion Unit (OCU) for the particular aircraft type and the reserve squadron has a mobilisation role.

Royal Air Force Regiment

1 Sqn RAF Regt	RAF Laarbruch	Ground Defence (closure 99)
2 Sqn RAF Regt	RAF Honnington	Ground Defence
3 Sqn RAF Regt	RAF Aldergrove	Ground Defence
15 Sqn RAF Regt	RAF Leeming	Rapier

26 Sqn RAF Regt	**RAF Laarbruch**	**Rapier**
27 Sqn RAF Regt	RAF Leuchars	Rapier (closure 99)
34 Sqn RAF Regt	RAF Akrotiri	Ground Defence/Light Armour
37 Sqn RAF Regt	RAF Bruggen	Rapier
48 Sqn RAF Regt	RAF Lossiemouth	Rapier
63 (QCS) Sqn	RAF Uxbridge	Ground Defence & Ceremonial
RAF Regt Depot	RAF Honnington	Training & Administration

Royal Auxiliary Air Force Regiment

1310 Wing RAuxAF Regt	RAF Honnington	HQ Unit
2503 Sqn RAuxAF Regt	RAF Waddington	Ground Defence
2620 Sqn RAuxAF Regt	RAF Marham	Ground Defence
2622 Sqn RAuxAF Regt	RAF Lossiemouth	Ground Defence
2624 Sqn RAuxAF Regt	RAF Brize Norton	Ground Defence
2625 Sqn RAuxAF Regt	RAF St Mawgan	Ground Defence

Flying Training

JEFTS	RAF Topcliffe	Civilian Aircraft
1 Flying Training School	RAF Linton-on-Ouse	Tucano
2 Flying Training School	RAF Shawbury	Gazelle/Wessex
3 Flying Training School	RAF Linton-on-Ouse	Tucano

Advanced Flying Training

4 Flying Training School	RAF Valley	Hawk
6 Flying Training School	RAF Cranwell	JP/Tucano/Hawk/ Bulldog Jetstream/Dominie
Central Flying School	RAF Cranwell	Tucano/Bulldog/ Hawk
Central Flying School	RAF Shawbury	Gazelle
Search & Rescue Training Unit	RAF Valley	Wessex
Sea King Training Unit	RAF St Mawgan	Sea King

British Airline Fleets

In an emergency, the Government has the power to enlist the assistance of the United Kingdom's civil airline fleets. In total there appear to be 34 registered airlines operating approximately 650 x fixed wing passenger and transport aircraft. The largest of these airlines is British Airways with some 50,000 employees operating about 240 aircraft, carrying on average about 27-28 million passengers and about half a million tons of freight per year.

Other major British airlines include Air UK with 28 aircraft. Britannia Airways the world's largest charter airline with 33 aircraft and carrying about 7 million passengers per year. British Midland Airways with 31 aircraft and Virgin Atlantic with 16 aircraft.

The composition of British Airway's fleet as at 1 January 1996 was as follows:

Aircraft	Total	Future Deliveries	Options
Concorde	7		
Boeing 747-100	15		
Boeing 747-200	16		
Boeing 747-400	25	36	22
Boeing 777		15	15
Tristar 1 and 100	5		
MD DC-10-30	7		
Boeing 767-300	20	8	9
Boeing 757-200	42	3	1
Airbus 320	10		
Boeing 737-200	39		
Boeing 737-300	3		
Boeing 737-400	32	6	10
BAC 1-11-500	6		
BAe ATP	14		6
Totals	241	68	63

Air Force Board

The routine management of the Royal Air Force is the Responsibility of the Air Force Board, the composition of which is shown in the next diagram:

Air Force Board
The Secretary of State for Defence

Minister of State (Armed Forces)	Chief of the Air Staff
Minister of State (Defence Procurement)	Air Member for Personnel
Under Secretary of State (Armed Forces)	Controller of Aircraft
Under Secretary of State Air	Member for Logistics
(Defence Procurement)	AOC Strike Command
2nd Permanant Under Secretary of State	Assistant Chief of Air Staff

Decisions made by the Defence Council or the Air Force Board are implemented by the air staff at various headquarters world-wide. The Chief of the Air Staff is the officer ultimately responsible for the Royal Air Force's contribution to the national defence effort. He maintains control through the AOC (Air Officer Commanding), and the staff branches of each of these headquarters.

Chief of The Air Staff (As at 1 Jan 1996)

Air Chief Marshal Sir Michael Graydon GCB CDE ADC FRAeS
Air Chief Marshal Graydon was born in Kew, Surrey, in October 1938 and was educated at Wycliffe College prior to entering the Royal Air Force College, Cranwell as a flight cadet in 1957 and being commissioned into the Royal Air Force in December 1959.

After training he completed a tour as a Qualified Flying Instructor with the Fleet Air Arm before embarking on a career as a fighter pilot with successive tours on Lightning aircraft with Nos 56, 226 OCU and again 56 Sqn, the latter as a flight commander. He was Lightning display pilot for Fighter Command in 1965/6 and in NEAF 1967/8, and was awarded the Queen's Commendation for Valuable Service in the Air in 1967. A short tour at Headquarters 11 Group was followed by attendance at the Royal Air Force Staff College, Bracknell after which he was appointed Personal Staff Officer to the Deputy Commander-in-Chief Allied Forces Central Europe at Brunssum in Holland

On returning to the United Kingdom in 1973, Air Chief Marshal Graydon spent two years in the Operations (Joint Warfare) Directorate of the Ministry of Defence before attending the National Defence College, Latimer. He commanded No 11 Squadron from 1977 to 1979 followed by an appointment as Military Assistant to the Chief of the Defence Staff. In 1981, Air Chief Marshal Graydon was appointed to command Royal Air Force Leuchars, followed by command of Royal Air Force Stanley in the Falkland Islands. He was made a Commander of the Order of the British Empire in January 1984, and attended the Royal College of Defence Studies in the same year. He then became Senior Staff Officer at Headquarters 11 Group before becoming Assistant Chief of Staff Policy at Supreme Headquarters Allied Powers Europe in July 1986.

Air Chief Marshal Graydon assumed command of Royal Air Force Support Command on 5 April 1989 and was made Knight Commander of the Order of Bath in June 1989. On promotion to Air Chief Marshal, in May 1991, he became Commander-in-Chief United Kingdom Air Forces and Air Officer Commanding-in- Chief Strike Command. He was appointed Chief of the Air Staff and Air Aide de Camp to HM The Queen on 6 November 1992.
Air Chief Marshal Graydon has flown some 4000 hrs mainly in Fighter aircraft.

149

Chain of Command

On the 1st April 1994 the Royal Air Force was reorganised into 3 major groupings with the resultant "Chain of Command" as follows:

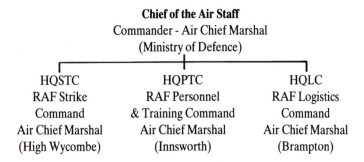

Chief of the Air Staff
Commander - Air Chief Marshal
(Ministry of Defence)

HQSTC	HQPTC	HQLC
RAF Strike	RAF Personnel	RAF Logistics
Command	& Training Command	Command
Air Chief Marshal	Air Chief Marshal	Air Chief Marshal
(High Wycombe)	(Innsworth)	(Brampton)

Strike Command

From its headquarters at RAF High Wycombe, Strike Command now controls all of the United Kingdom's front-line aircraft world-wide. Its assets include fighters, strike/attack, transport and maritime aircraft and helicopters

Strike Command is also an essential part of the NATO organisation and the Air Officer Commanding-in-Chief Strike Command (AOCinC STC) holds the dual appointment of Commander-in-Chief United Kingdom Air Forces (CINCUKAIR) - a NATO appointment.

As the commander of Strike Command the AOCinC is responsible for the day to day national peacetime operations of the Command. As CINCUKAIR he is also responsible to the Supreme Allied Commander Europe (SACEUR) for the defence of the UK Air Defence Region (UKADR) and the provision of combat-ready air forces to support other NATO commands.

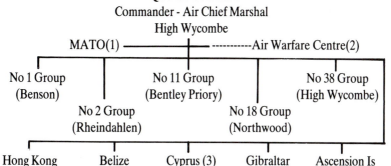

HQ Strike Command
Commander - Air Chief Marshal
High Wycombe

MATO(1) ———————————— ----------Air Warfare Centre(2)

No 1 Group		No 11 Group		No 38 Group
(Benson)		(Bentley Priory)		(High Wycombe)
	No 2 Group		No 18 Group	
	(Rheindahlen)		(Northwood)	

Hong Kong   Belize   Cyprus (3)   Gibraltar   Ascension Is

Notes:

(1) MATO stands for Military Air Traffic Organisation. (2) The Air Warfare Centre (formerly CTTO) is responsible for the Tornado F3 OEU and the SAOEU.

(3) Cyprus has Group Status within Strike Command. (4) Groups are normally commanded by Air Vice Marshals although the commander of 18 Group is an Air Marshal.

In general these 5 Groups are responsible for:

1 Group	-	Strike/Attack/Army Support
2 Group	-	Germany/ARRC Support
11 Group	-	Air Defence
18 Group	-	Maritime Patrol EW and SAR
38 Group	-	Air Transport, Communications & AAR

During mid 1995 Strike Command controlled about 5,000 civilians and 40,000 servicemen and women - over half of the present strength of the Royal Air Force and operates some 800 aircraft. The personnel and aircraft are spread through some 200 units of various sizes, the majority of which are in the United Kindom. Strike Command is based upon five core groups:

No 1 Group

HQ No 1 Group
RAF Benson - Strike/Attack/Army Support

Harrier	Tornado	Jaguar	Chinook	Puma/Wessex
1 Sqn	2 Sqn GR1A	6 Sqn	7 Sqn	33 Sqn
20 Sqn(R)	13 Sqn GRIA	16 Sqn(R)		60 Sqn
	15 (R) Sqn GR1	41 Sqn		72 Sqn
	TTTE	54 Sqn		230 Sqn
				27 Sqn(R)

No 1 Group has the following RAF Regiment Squarons under commnd:

No 2 Sqn RAF Regt - Honnington - Field Squadron
No 3 Sqn RAF Regt - Aldergrove - Field Squadron

No 2 Group

HQ No 2 Group
Rheindahlen - Germany/ARRC Support

Harrier	Tornado	Puma/Chinook
3 Sqn	9 Sqn GR1	18 Sqn
4 Sqn	14 Sqn GR1	
	17 Sqn GR1 & 31 Sqn GR1	

Low level air defence of airfields is provided by Rapier equipped Air Defence squadrons of the RAF Regiment. No 2 Group has the following RAF Regiment Squadrons under command:

No 1 Sqn RAF Regt	-	Laarbruch	-	Field Squadron
No 26 Sqn RAF Regt	-	Laarbruch	-	Rapier
No 37 Sqn RAF Regt	-	Bruggen	-	Rapier

No 2 Group also has the following under command:

RAF Decimomannu (Sardinia)	-	Air Combat & Weapons Training
RAF Nordhorn	-	Air Weapons Training Facility
RAF (Hospital)	-	Wegberg
RAF Signals Unit	-	Bruggen
RAF Signals Unit	-	Rheindahlen

Note: RAF Laarbruch closes in 1999

No 11 Group

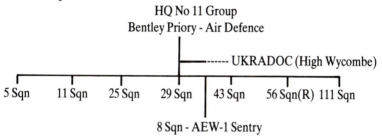

HQ No 11 Group
Bentley Priory - Air Defence

------ UKRADOC (High Wycombe)

5 Sqn   11 Sqn   25 Sqn   29 Sqn   43 Sqn   56 Sqn(R) 111 Sqn

8 Sqn - AEW-1 Sentry

Note: With the obvious exception of 8 Sqn all of these Sqns are equipped with Tornado F3.

Low level air defence of airfields is provided by Rapier equipped Air Defence squadrons of the RAF Regiment. No 11 Group has the following RAF Regiment Squadrons under command:

No 15 Sqn RAF Regt	-	Leeming	-	Rapier
No 27 Sqn RAF Regt	-	Leuchars	-	Rapier
No 48 Sqn RAF Regt	-	Lossiemouth	-	Rapier

Also included under command No 11 Group are:

Tornado F3 OEU	-	Coningsby
Sentry Training Squadron	-	Waddington
Battle of Britian Memorial Flight	-	Coningsby

No 18 Group

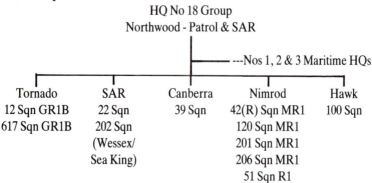

HQ No 18 Group
Northwood - Patrol & SAR

---Nos 1, 2 & 3 Maritime HQs

Tornado	SAR	Canberra	Nimrod	Hawk
12 Sqn GR1B	22 Sqn	39 Sqn	42(R) Sqn MR1	100 Sqn
617 Sqn GR1B	202 Sqn		120 Sqn MR1	
	(Wessex/		201 Sqn MR1	
	Sea King)		206 Sqn MR1	
			51 Sqn R1	

No 18 Group has the following units under command:

SARTU (Search & Rescue Training Unit) - Valley
SKTU (Sea King Training Unit) - St Mawgan

The main activities of No 18 Group are maritime surface and subsurface surveillance, search and rescue (SAR) and regular patrolling of the North Sea oil and gas installations, and fishery limits. Tasks are controlled from the Air Headquarters at Northwood, Middlesex. In war, the Nimrods would operate under the Supreme Allied Commander Atlantic (SACLANT), the AOC No 18 Group holding the NATO post of Commander Maritime Air Eastern Atlantic (COMMAIREASTLANT). As such, his main tasks would be to provide maritime strike/attack, maritime reconnaissance and anti-submarine support for naval operations and in protection of allied merchant shipping.

The major headquarters for co-ordinating this activity are:

No 1 Maritime HQ - Northwood
No 2 Maritime HQ - Pitrivie
No 3 Maritime HQ - St Mawgan

The UK MoD recently announced the opening of a Joint Maritime

Communications Centre (JMCC) at St Mawgan in Cornwall. When the headquarters is operational in 1996, some 400 personnel will be associated with the JMCC of whom about 50% will be US Navy. Of about 200 UK personnel, 50% will be from the Royal Navy and 50% from the RAF. The UK MoD will pay for the JMCC building and the US will pay for the equipment. The JMCC comprises a buried, hardened communications building approximately 70 metres square within the perimeter of RAF St Mawgan. The centre will be integrated within the existing RAF fixed communications system, and will include two additional satellite ground terminals, each approximately 3 metres in diameter, also sited within the station boundary.

No 18 Group controls Search and Rescue (SAR) through the Rescue Coordination Centres at Plymouth and Edinburgh. The Group's search and rescue Sea King and Wessex helicopters with, where appropriate, the Nimrods and marine craft units, are frequently engaged in rescue work and mercy flights, saving several hundred lives each year. The Group is also responsible for photographic reconnaissance cover using Canberra PR9. The Canberra PR unit also undertakes photographic surveys for the Ministry of Defence and other Government Departments in many parts of the world.

No 38 Group

HQ No 38 Group
High Wycombe - Air Transport - Communications - AAR

VC10	Hercules	32 (Royal) Sqn	Tristar
10 Sqn C1/C1K	24 Sqn	HS125/146	216 Sqn
101 Sqn K2/K3	30 Sqn	Queens Flight	(Brize Norton
(Brize Norton	47 Sqn	(Northolt)	
	70 Sqn		
	57(R) Sqn		
	(Lyneham)		

Air Defence

One of Strike Command's main responsibilities is the United Kingdom Air Defence Region(UKADR). AOC Strke Command delegates day-to-day operational responsibility to the AOC No 11 Group, and the Group's task is to provide early warning of air attack against the UKADR, to provide fighter and missile defences and the associated ground control system, fighter co-ordination with Royal Naval Ships operating in adjacent waters and to maintain the integrity of UK air space in war.

The UK control and reporting centres are linked with other elements of the NATO Air Defence Ground Environment (NADGE) and with the Ballistic Missile Early Warning Systems (BMEWS) station at Fylingdales, Yorkshire, which is networked with the US operated BMEWS at Thule ((Greenland) and Clear (Alaska). By extending high-level radar cover some 3,000 miles across Eastern Europe, Fylingdales would give advance warning of intermediate range ballistic missiles launched against the UK and Western Europe, and of inter-continental ballistic missiles against the North American continent. Fylingdales also tracks satellites and space debris.

The UK Air Defence Region (UKADR) Radar Reporting Network

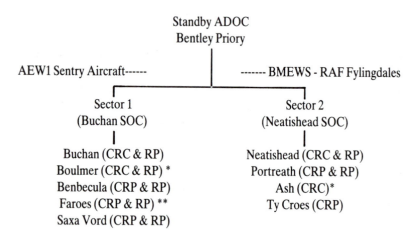

United Kingdom Region
Air Defence Operations Centre (UKRADOC)
High Wycombe

Standby ADOC
Bentley Priory

AEW1 Sentry Aircraft------   ------ BMEWS - RAF Fylingdales

Sector 1   Sector 2
(Buchan SOC)   (Neatishead SOC)

Buchan (CRC & RP)   Neatishead (CRC & RP)
Boulmer (CRC & RP) *   Portreath (CRP & RP)
Benbecula (CRP & RP)   Ash (CRC)*
Faroes (CRP & RP) **   Ty Croes (CRP)
Saxa Vord (CRP & RP)

* Denotes Reserve SOC
** Operated by the Royal Danish Air Force

In Reserve - STC Mobile Radar Reserve (144 Signals Unit)

Key: SOC   -   Sector Operations Centre
        CRC   -   Control Reporting Centre
        CRP   -   Control Reporting Point
        RP   -   Reporting Point

I-UKADGE (Improved- UK Air Defence Ground Environment) is the communications system upon which the air defences depend for their operational effectiveness. The system is fully automated. Computerised data exchange and information from a number of sources such as radars, ships and aircraft is moved around the system on a number of routes to minimise the disruptive effects of enemy action. Generally speaking if a command bunker or radar is rendered inoperable, the system will automatically switch to another node allowing a secure, free and uninterupted flow of information. ICCS (Integrated Command and Control System) provides the Commanders and air defence staff the information gathered in the system and UNITER brings together all the nodes on a digital network.

JTIDS (Joint Tactical Information Distribution System) is a secure communications network. The MoD has ordered 60 terminals and the majority of these will equip 2 x Tornado F3 squadrons and the AEW1 Sentry aircraft. Military Air Traffic Operations (MATO) has Group status within Strike Command and is based at Hillingdon House, Uxbridge. It is co-located with Civil Air Traffic Operations (CATO) under a Joint Field Commander (JFC - Air Commodore - AOC MATO) who is responsible for the joint implementation of National Air Traffic Services (NATS) policy for the control of civil and military aircraft in the UK.

AOCMATO is operationally responsible to the Controller MATS for all military ATC services in UK airspace other than those provided at airfields. MATO is administered by Strike Command in peacetime and controlled by CINCUKAIR in war.

Air Warfare Centre (AWC)
The Air Warfare Centre is responsible for formulating tactical doctrine and conducting operational trials. Formed from the old CTTO, DAW, EWOSE, ORB and OEUs the AWC also maintains liaison with MoD research establishments and industry, and close contact with RAF operational commands as well as with the Royal Navy, Army and Allied air forces.

The AWC is administered by HQ Strike Command, but is responsible jointly to the Assistant Chief of Air Staff, and to the Commander-in-Chief for the conduct of trials, and development of tactics for all Royal Air Force operational aircraft. Branches and locations of the AWC are as follows:

Operational Doctrine (OD&T)	Cranwell & High Wycombe
Tactics (TD&T)	Waddington
Electronic Warfare (EWOS)	Waddington
Operational Analysis (OA)	High Wycombe, Waddington & Cranwell
Operational Testing & Evaluation (OT&E)	Boscombe Down, Conningsby, Odiham & Ash

RAF Personnel & Training Command (RAF PTC)
HQ PTC controls all personnel aspects ranging from conditions of service, recruiting, training, education, manning, career management, resettlement and pensions. The new headquarters also deals with all policy matters relating to Medical, Dental, Legal and Chaplaincy. Final staff numbers will probably be in the areas of 1,500 with a split of about 55% civilians and 45% service personnel.

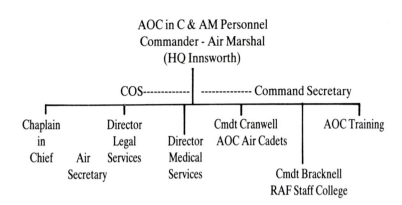

AOC in C & AM Personnel
Commander - Air Marshal
(HQ Innsworth)

COS------------- | -------------- Command Secretary

| Chaplain in Chief | Director Legal Services | Director Medical Services | Cmdt Cranwell AOC Air Cadets | AOC Training |
| Air Secretary | | | Cmdt Bracknell RAF Staff College | |

Chief of Staff's Branch (COS)

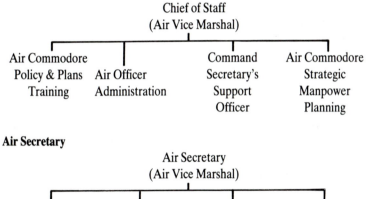

Chief of Staff
(Air Vice Marshal)

| Air Commodore Policy & Plans Training | Air Officer Administration | Command Secretary's Support Officer | Air Commodore Strategic Manpower Planning |

Air Secretary

Air Secretary
(Air Vice Marshal)

| Director Personnel Management O & AA | Director Personnel Management Amn & CRF | Director Information Services | AOC & Director Recruiting & Selection |

Director Medical Services

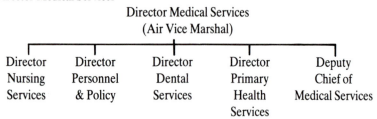

Director Medical Services
(Air Vice Marshal)

Director Nursing Services	Director Personnel & Policy	Director Dental Services	Director Primary Health Services	Deputy Chief of Medical Services

Air Officer Training

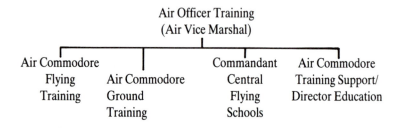

Air Officer Training
(Air Vice Marshal)

Air Commodore Flying Training	Air Commodore Ground Training	Commandant Central Flying Schools	Air Commodore Training Support/ Director Education

Note: We believe that the Red Arrows will be under the control of AOC Flying Training

RAF Logistic Command (RAF LC)

HQ LC located at the Brampton/Wyton complex has about 4,000 personnel, about 50% of whom are civilians managing a cash budget of some 1.8 billion, or about half a million pounds per staff member annually. The headquarters "core" staff numbers about 200 and the vast majority of the staff are involved in the direct management and control of maintenance activities such as provisioning, storage, distribution, logistic operations, information systems and communications.

RAF LC Organisation

The following is a guide to what we believe is the current organisation for RAF Logistic Command.

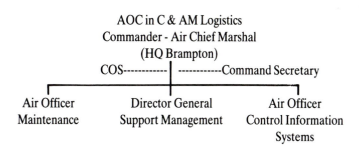

AOC in C & AM Logistics
Commander - Air Chief Marshal
(HQ Brampton)
COS------------ | ------------Command Secretary

Air Officer
Maintenance

Director General
Support Management

Air Officer
Control Information
Systems

Chief of Staff's Branch (COS)

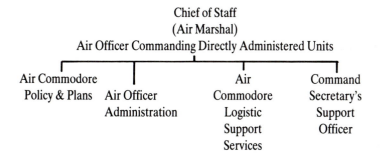

Chief of Staff
(Air Marshal)
Air Officer Commanding Directly Administered Units

Air Commodore
Policy & Plans

Air Officer
Administration

Air
Commodore
Logistic
Support
Services

Command
Secretary's
Support
Officer

Air Officer Maintenance

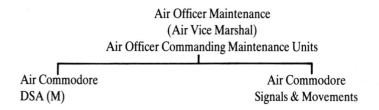

Air Officer Maintenance
(Air Vice Marshal)
Air Officer Commanding Maintenance Units

Air Commodore
DSA (M)

Air Commodore
Signals & Movements

161

Director General Support Management

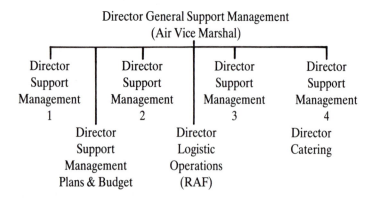

Air Officer Commanding Signals Units

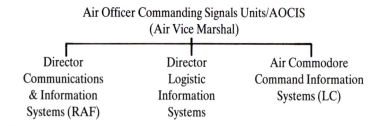

Maintenance

The maintenance functions at Logistic Command can be divided into aero systems engineering (those engineering functions concerned with aircraft) signals and movements. RAFLC provides aircraft engineering support for the RAF, and for fixed wing aircraft of the Royal Navy and Army Air Corps.

Scheduled major maintenance, rectifications, reconditioning and Modification of a wide variety of aircraft are undertaken for tasks beyond the normal capability of operational stations.

Maintenance Units (MUs) also hold reserve stocks of fixed wing aircraft, which they prepare for storage and maintenance against deterioration.

Continuous effort is devoted to the improvement of maintenance facilities, the introduction of improved tools and better working methods to increase efficiency and reduce costs.

Work on aircraft is carried out at RAF St Athan. The engineering unit at St Athan, the largest in the RAF, is manned jointly by service personnel and civilians, with an Aircraft Servicing Wing and a General Engineering Wing. The former has been engaged for many years on the maintenance of Harriers, Phantoms and Tornados with the capacity to work on 58 aircraft at any one time.

In July 1992, the engineering facilities at RAF Abingdon were concentrated at St Athan. This move brought responsibility for the major maintenance and Modification of Jaguar, Hawk and VC10 aircraft and the Repair and Salvage Squadron, which is responsible for salvaging crashed RAF, Army and Navy fixed wing aircraft in most parts of the world and carries out aircraft recovery for the Department of Transport. In addition to crash recovery, the Repair and Salvage Squadron also sends teams of tradesmen to operational stations to undertake Modifications and repairs that are beyond the capacity of unit personnel, but do not necessitate the aircraft being returned to a maintenance unit. In realistic scenarios, aircraft battle damage repair techniques are formulated and tested for all of the British Services, and some 18 other nations have benefited from such training.

No 30 Maintenance Unit (30 MU) at RAF Sealand near Chester, is the main engineering unit for airborne electronic and instrument equipment. Large workshops and test facilities are laid out on production lines to enable the unit to service more than 100,000 items of airborne radio, radar, electrical, instrument and missile engineering equipment a year. The unit also provides a test equipment calibration service and manufactures test equipment, aircraft cables and looms.

The RAF Armament Support Unit (RAFASUPU) at RAF Wittering houses the RAF Explosive Ordnance Disposal (EOD) Squadron which is responsible for all aspects of RAF EOD training and trials, as well as actual clearance operations. RAFASUPU also trains aircrew and groundcrew in all aspects of special weapons functions and moves weapons as required.

In addition to the major aircraft engineering tasks, RAF LC repairs almost any kind of equipment when it is expedient and economical to do so Parachutes, ground equipment, furniture and domestic equipment are typical examples. There are large workshops at each of the Equipment Supply Depots that undertake the Modification, repair and servicing of almost any item of equipment that comes from units in an unservicable condition. A considerable sum of money is saved by this repair facility, enabling requirements for scarce equipment to be met more quickly.

Signals

The units controlled by the RAF LC Signals Staff based at RAF Henlow, are responsible for the support aspects of telecommunications, ground radio repair and signals engineering. The Signal Staff are responsible for operating the RAF element of the Defence Communications Network (DCN) and acts as a consultant to MoD, other RAF Commands and to Allied Air Forces for all aspects of communications. The Signal Staff are also responsible for the Henlow based Communications-Electronic Multi Disciplinary Group, responsible to the MoD for support authority functions in respect of telegraphic automatic routing equipment, telegraph, ground radio and ground radar equipments for the three services and other organisations.

Communications operating responsibilities fall into four categories. First, there is a large complex of HF transmitter and receiver facilities in the UK, including communications centres with automatic message routing equipment. Operations include those on behalf of Strike Command, the Military Air Traffic Organisation, NATO and the Meteorological Office.

Second, LC operates message relay centres, both automatic and manual and also manages the RAF's General Purpose Telephone network. The RAF has also procured a fixed telecommunications network called Boxer which will save the increasing expense of renting lines from the private sector. Command operating procedures are monitored on all networks to ensure high standards are achieved and maintained. To reduce risk of compromise, all RAF communications facilities designed to carry classified information are checked for communications electrical security by Command staff.

Thirdly, the main operation of the Skynet Satellite Communications System, which offers overseas formations telegraphed, data and speech communications, is controlled by the Command. In February 1994, a contract for some £300 million was awarded for the development, production and delivery of 2 x Skynet 4 Stage 2 military communications satellites. These will replace the existing Skynet satellites as they approach the end of their operational life, and will enter service in 1998. In addition, a management service for the NATO 4 series of satellites is provided.

Fourth, the deep maintenance and repair of ground radio and radar equipments is carried out by the Ground Radio Servicing Centre (GRSC) at RAF North Luffenham. This includes radars, radio navigation aids and point-to-point and ground-to-air communications. The Command also provides an antenne systems maintenance service on a world wide basis, embracing the fields of communications, radar and navigation aids. The men required for this highly specialised work are trained by the Command at the Aerial Erector School at RAF Digby.

The Command's responsibilities for electrical engineering range over the entire field of communications equipment, air traffic control and defence radar systems and ground based navigational equipment. They include feasibility studies, project management, design, development, manufacture, refurbishment, installation and commissioning of the majority of communications equipment procured by the MOD(PE).

AOC Signals has a large engineering design staff of engineers, technicians and draughtsmen. Manufacturing resources include a general mechanical engineering and calibration capacity at RAF Henlow and, at RAF Wyton, a facility for the systems design, development and installation of certain airborne signals role equipment.

Supply

The size and composition of the Logistic Command supply units vary according to their respective functions, from equipment supply depots to comparatively small petroleum supply depots. The equipment supply depots hold nearly one and a half million different types of technical and domestic equipment. Quantities vary from a few months to several years consumption, according to whether this item can be replenished quickly or can be bought in economic quantities only when the manufacturer is tooled-up to produce it. The number of different items held in stock is greater, and the variety wider, than would be found in any one civilian firm in the UK. Stocks are at present distributed amongst four large depots located at Stafford, Carlisle, Quedgeley and Chilmark.

Over the years, the techniques of stock recording and stock location and the speedy handling of stores items have continually improved. Today the highest priority demands for equipment are fully processed within six hours of their receipt at the depot for delivery throughout the world. This service, which operates 24 hours a day every day of the year, is supported by one of the UK's most powerful computers located at the RAF Supply Control Centre. It is here that a central record of the location and quantity of nearly every item of equipment held throughout the RAF is located.

The equipment supply depots and about 100 stations at home and overseas are linked to the Supply Control Centre. As a result, the computer is able to direct any urgently required item of equipment from the appropriate depot or, if quicker, to be transferred from another RAF station. It also provides accurate consumption information to ensure that the item is purchased in the most cost effective quantities.

Operationally, Logistic Command also supports major force deployments through the Tactical Supply Wing. Based at RAF Stafford, this organisation is equipped to move at very short notice to provide a range of support facilities, including fuel and spares, anywhere in the world.

Overseas Bases

Strike Command has responsibility for all RAF bases overseas, including the units in Germany, the Mediterranean, Far East, and North America.

AHQ Cyprus has Group status within Strike Command. In Cyprus, there is a resident squadron of Wessex helicopters, some of which support UNFICYP with the remainder in the SAR role, while facilities exist at RAF Akrotiri to support aircraft detached from UK. In addition, an RAF Regiment Squadron is deployed at Akrotiri for airfield defence.

RAF Gibraltar is directly administered by HQ 18 Group. The airfield is operated by the RAF, although there is no resident squadron. Strike Command controls RAF units for administrative and engineering purposes in Hong Kong where there is a squadron of Wessex helicopters.

In North America there is a Strike Command detachment at Offutt Air Force Base, Nebraska, to support overseas training detachments, and a permanent unit is established at Goose Bay in Labrador for a similar purpose.

Strike Command also provides a Tornado Air Defence Unit, a flight of Hercules transport/tankers and Sea King and Chinook helicopters in the Falkland Islands. In early 1994, there were Strike Command units operating in support of the United Nations in Saudi Arabia, Bahrain, Turkey and the former Yugoslavia.

During operations and exercises, aircraft often visit overseas airfields where no regular RAF ground handling organisation exists. For this purpose, the Group has a Mobile Air Movement Squadron (MAMS) at RAF Lyneham, which provides teams who are expert in all aspects of loading and unloading aircraft. The MAMS teams log a large number of flying hours annually and are normally on the first aircraft in, and last aircraft out in any major overseas operation, exercise or relief operation.

RAF Station Organisation
An indication of the manner in which an RAF Station might be organised is as follows. Our example is an RAF Station with 3 x Tornado GR1 flying squadrons - each with 12 x aircraft. The 36 aircraft will have cost at least £720 million in total purchase costs, and the combined running costs for the operation of these three squadrons will be in the region of some £80 million pounds per annum.

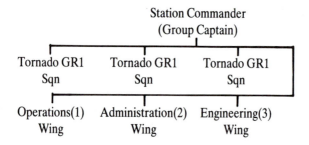

Notes: (1) Ops Wing; (2) Admin Wing; (3) Eng Wing; (4) Expect the commanders of the Tornado Sqns to be Wing Commanders aged between 34-40 Ops, Admin and Eng Wings will almost certainly be commanded by Wing Commanders from their respective branch specialities - these Wing Commanders will probably be a little older than the commanders of the flying squadrons.

Flying Squadron Organisation

Note: (1 These departental leaders hae responsibiliy for weapons, airframes, propulsion, electronics, flight guidance and control systems, communications, automatic navigation and attack controls and report to the squadron commander.

Administration Wing Organisation.

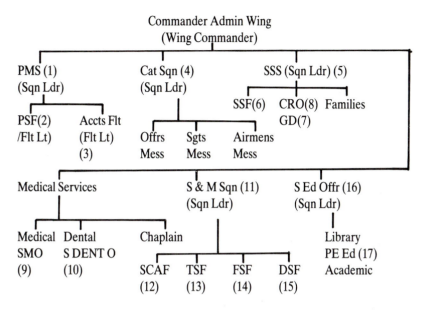

Notes: (1) Personnel Management Squadron; (2) Personal Services Flight; (3) Accounts Flight; (4) Catering Sqn; (5) Station Services Sqn; (6) Station Services Flight; (7) General Duties Flight; (8) Community Relations Officer (9) Senior Medical Officer; (10) Senior Dental Officer; (11) Supply & Movements Sqn; (12) Supply Control & Accounts Flight; (13) Technical Supply Flight; (14) Forward Supply Flight; (15) Domestic Supply Flight; (16) Senior Education Officer; (17) Physicial Education.

Operations Wing Organisation

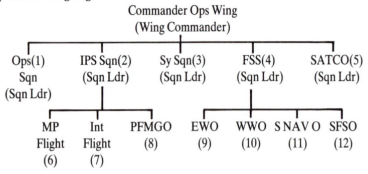

Notes: (1) Operations Sqn; (2) Intelligence & Planning Sqn; (3) Security Sqn - includes RAF Police & Station Defence Personnel; (4) Flying Support Sqn; (5) Senior Air Traffic Control Officer; (6) Mission Plans Flight; (7) Intelligence Flight; (8) Pre-flight Message Generation Officer; (9) Electronic Warfare Officer; (10) Wing Weapon Officer; (11) Senior Navigation Officer; (12) Station Safety Officer.

Engineering Wing

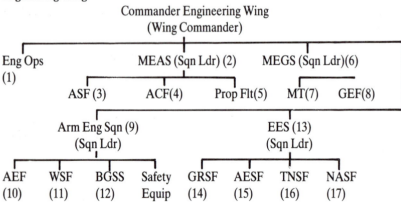

Notes: (1) Engineering Ops; (2) Mechanical Engineering Aircraft Sqn; (3) Aircraft Servicing Flight; (4) Aircraft Components Flight; (5) Propulsion Flight; (6) Mechanical Engineering Ground Squadron; (7) Mechanical Transport; (8)

General Engineering Flight; (9) Armament Engineering Sqn; (10) Armament Engineering Flight; (11) Weapon Storage Flight; (12) Bomb Group Section (13) Electrical Engineering Squadron; (14) Ground Radio Servicing Fliight; (15) Avionics Electrical Systems Flight; (16) Tornado Navigation Systems Flight; (17) Navigation and Attack Systems Flight.

Operational Conversion Unit (OCU)

The RAF has a number of OCU's designed to train pilots for front line squadron service as follows:

Tornado OCU	25 x Tornado GR1	RAF Lossiemouth	(15 Reserve Sqn)
Tornado F3 OCU	24 x Tornado F3	RAF Coningsby	(56 Reserve Sqn)
Jaguar OCU	10 x Jaguar	RAF Lossiemouth	(16 Reserve Sqn)
Harrier OCU	16 x Harrier	RAF Wittering	(20 Reserve Sqn)
Nimrod OCU	5 x Nimrod MR2	RAF Kinloss	(42 Reserve Sqn)
Helicopter OCU	4 x Chinook; 5 x Puma	RAF Odiham	(27 Reseve Sqn)
Hercules OCU	5 x Hercules	RAF Lyneham	(57 Reserve Sqn)
VC-10/Tristar	As required	RAF Brize Norton	

The organisation of an OCU is obviously tailored to fit the size of the aircraft fleet being supported. As an example No 56 Reserve Sqn (Tornado F3 OCU) is organised along the following lines:

Commander OCU - (Wing Commander)

A Flight	B Flight	C Flight	D Flight

A and B Flights provide flying training with about 23 x staff crews and 12 x student crews. C Flight is a standards flight - training instructors, and D Flight provides simulators and a dome air combat trainer.

Royal Air Force Major Equipment Summary

Aircraft available for immediate operations as at 1 January 1996 - we estimate some 560 combat aircraft capable of delivering missiles or ordnance.

129 x Tornado GR1; 26 x Tornado GR1A; 127 x Tornado F3; 80 x Harrier; 124 x Hawk; 56 x Jaguar GR1A; 16 x Jaguar T2A; 3 x Nimrod R1; 26 x Nimrod M2; 7 x

-3D Sentry; 16 x Canberra; 9 x VC10 K2/K3; 10 x VC10 C1/C1K; 9 x Tristar K1/KC1/C2; 58 x Hercules; 12 x HS125; 3 x BAe 146; 60 x Chipmunk; 110 x Bulldog; 126 x Tucano; 18 x Dominie; 11 x Jetstream; 28 x Gazelle; 32 x Chinook; 19 x Sea King; 54 x Wessex; 37 x Puma.

Tornado GR-1

In Service With:

9 Sqn	12 x Tornado GR1 (1)	RAF Bruggen
12 Sqn	12 x Tornado GR1B (1)	RAF Lossiemouth
14 Sqn	12 x Tornado GR1 (1)	RAF Bruggen
17 Sqn	12 x Tornado GR1 (1)	RAF Bruggen
31 Sqn	12 x Tornado GR1 (1)	RAF Bruggen
617 Sqn	12 x Tornado GR1B (1)	RAF Lossiemouth
15 (R) Sqn	16 x Tornado GR1 (6)	RAF Lossiemouth
TTTE*	14 x Tornado GR1 (2)	RAF Cottesmore

* TTTE - Trinational Tornado Training Establishment.
Figures in brackets refer to In Use Reserve (IUR) aircraft.

Crew 2; Wingspan (open) 13.9m; Wingspan (swept) 8.6m; Height 5.9m; Length 16.7m; Max Weapon Load 7,250kg; Max Take Off Weight 27,900kg; Max Speed Mach 2.2 (1452 mph); Max Ferry Range approx 3,900kms; Armament 2 x 27mm Mauser Cannon, 3 x weapon points under fuselage, 4 x weapon points under wings; Engines 2 x Turbo-Union RB 199-34R Turbofans; Required Runway Length approx 900m

The Tornado GR-1 is an aircraft jointly developed by the UK, West Germany and Italy under a collaborative agreement and manufactured by a consortium of companies formed under the name of Panavia. The Tornado is the most

numerous and important aircraft in the RAF inventory and the GR-1 operates in the strike/attack and reconnaissance roles. The first prototype flew in 1974 and the first RAF Squadron equipped with the GR-1 became operational in 1982.

The GR-1 is capable of of carrying both nuclear and conventional weapons at tree-top height, in all weathers, by day or by night. It has a very advanced terrain following radar and sophisticated electronic countermeasures which assist in penetrating hostile airspace. For self-defence a 27mm cannon and Sidewinder missiles are carried. The Tornado GR-1A is the reconnaissance version of the aircraft, and the GR-1B is an aircraft Modified to allow the Sea Eagle missile to be used to its full capability.

During the Gulf War Tornado GR1s were amongst the first aircraft in action from 17th January 1991. Equipped with JP233 airfield denial weapons, 1,000 pound bombs and ALARM anti-radar missiles, GR1s attacked a number of the Iraqi Air Force's huge airfields. During the first week of operations the majority of the GR1 sorties were flown at low level and at night, an environment in which few other aircraft could operate.

By the end of the first week of operations the Iraqi Air Force was either in hiding in Iran or was trapped on damaged airfields. The overwhelming success of the offensive counter-air campaign against the Iraqi airfields created the opportunity to change Tornado tactics and, for the next three weeks, the GR1 force flew both day and night missions against a variety of interdiction targets, whilst continuing interval bombardment of Iraqi targets. With the air threat neutralised, the Tornado GR1 could now operate at medium level, above the reach of anti-aircraft artillery and using ballistic free fall 1,000 pound bombs.

The deployment of a squadron of Buccaneer aircraft equipped with Pavespike laser designators enabled the Tornado GR1s to use Laser Guided Bombs (LGBs) with great precision during daylight raids on interdiction and airfield targets. The GR1s capability was further enhanced with the deployment of a small number of aircraft fitted with the new Thermal Imaging Airborne Laser Designator (TIALD) which gave the Tornado GR1s a precision night attack capability. The final three weeks of the air war saw the Tornado GR1 force concentrating almost

173

exclusively on day and night precision attacks dropping LGBs from medium altitude.

A total of six GR1s were lost in action, five of which were involved in low or medium level attacks with 1,000 pound bombs and one that was flying a low level JP233 mission. During the war, the Tornado GR1 force flew 1,500 operational sorties divided almost equally between offensive counter air targets such as airfields and air defence sites, and interdiction targets such as bridges. Between them, Tornado GR1 and Jaguar GR1A's dropped some 100 x JP233 airfield denial weapons, 5,000 x 1,000 pound bombs, 1,000 x LGBs, 100 x ALARM missiles and 700 x Air to Ground Rockets onto Iraqi positions. The RAF deployed 48 x GR1 in the area during hostilities.

The first aircraft of the Tornado GR4 MLU version (mid life update) took off from British Aerospace (Wharton) for a 90 minute flight durng June 1993. The development contract for the MLU progamme was signedwith BAe in 1993 and includes introducing new equipment and updated avionics into the basic Tornado GR1 airframe. In addition, lessons from the Gulf War have been incorporated in the programme and it is believed that an improved thermal imaging laser designator pod and integrated global positioning system have been included. Funds of approximately £657 million are believed to have been allocated for the MLU with peak years of expenditure between 1996 and 2000.

Expect a Tornado GR1 Squadron to have 15 established crews.

Tornado GR1A

In Service With:

2 Sqn	12 x Tornado GR1A (1)	RAF Marham
13 Sqn	12 x Tornado GR1A (1)	RAF Marham

Note: Figures in brackets refer to In Use Reserve (IUR) aircraft.

The Torado GR1A is the Recce version of the Tornado and has what the RAF describes as "a unique day/night low level reconnaissance capability"

During the Gulf War, six Tornado GR1A aircraft, usually flying in pairs at night and at low level, flew some 140 operational sorties

Tornado F3

In Service With:

5 Sqn	12 x Tornado F3 (1)	RAF Coningsby
11 Sqn	15 x Tornado F3 (1)	RAF Leeming
25 Sqn	15 x Tornado F3 (1)	RAF Leeming
29 Sqn	12 x Tornado F3 (1)	RAF Coningsby
43 Sqn	13 x Tornado F3 (1)	RAF Leuchars
111 Sqn	13 x Tornado F3 (1)	RAF Leuchars
56 (R) Sqn	20 x Tornado F3 (1)	RAF Coningsby

Note: Figures in brackets refer to In Use Reserve (IUR) aircraft.

Crew 2; Wingspan (open) 13.9m; Wingspan (swept) 8.6m; Height 5.9m; Length 18.6m; Max Weapon Load 8,500kg; Max Take Off Weight 27,900kg; Max Speed Mach 2.2 (1452 mph); Armament 1 x 27mm Mauser Cannon, 4 x Sky Flash; 4 x AIL 9L Sidewinder; Engines 2 x Turbo-Union RB 199-34R-Mk104 Turbofans; Intercept Radius 1,850 km (subsonic) or 550 kms (supersonic)

The Tornado F3 is armed with 4 x semi-recessed Sky Flash, 4 x Sidewinder AIM 9L missiles and a single Mauser 27mm cannon and has about 80% commonality with the Tornado GR1. The main difference is the extended fuselage, longer range air intercept Foxhunter Radar (replacing the terrain following/ground mapping radar of the Tornado GR1) and the armmament. Extension of the fuselage provides additional space for avionics and an extra 900 litres of fuel.

The F3 was designed to meet the RAF's commitment for the air defence of the extensive UK Air Defence Region (UKADR). The aircraft has a long range autonomous capability that enables operations to be conducted some 350 nm away from bases in bad weather, in an ECM environment and opearing against muliple-targets at high or low level, which can be engaged at distances in excess of 20 nm. With tanker support the Tornado F3 Combat Air Patrol (CAP) time is increased from 2 hrs and 30mins to a loiter time of several hours.

The Air Defence Variant (ADV) of the Tornado from which the F3 was developed flew for the first time in October 1979, and the F3 will almost certainly stay in service until it is replaced by the European Fighter Aircraft (EFA) during the early part of the next century.

RAF Tornado F3s were sent to the Gulf in August 1990. By the end of hostilities on the 28th Feburary 1991, 18 x F3 aircraft had flown some 2,500 sorties during their deployment including 700 sorties during the period of hostilities. During 1993, the RAF has participated in NATO operations to enforce a No-Fly Zone over Bosnia as part of Operation Deny Flight and since mid 1993 an average of 8 x F-3 aircraft had been operating from airbases in Italy.

Expect a Tornado F3 Squadron to have between 16 and 20 established crews. In early 1994 Italy leased 24 x Tornado F3 from the UK to bridge the gap until the Eurofighter enters service.

Tornado in World Service (Original Procurement Figures)

	GR1/IDS	F2/F3/ADV	ECR/GR1A/Recce
UK	199	170	26
Germany	302	-	36
Italy	70	24 (leased from UK)	-
Saudi Arabia	48	24	-

RAF Tornado F-3 armed with 4 Sky Flash and 4 Sidewinder air to air missiles (British Aerospace).

Ground crew fitting a Sky Flash missile to a Tornado F-3 at RAF Leeming (P Info HQ RAF Logistics Command).

Aircraft in use by RAF Personnel & Training Command since 1990 (clockwise) Hawk; Chipmunk; Jet Provost; HS 125; Gazelle; Wessex; Jetstream; Tucano; Bulldog (P Info HQ RAF PTC).

179

An RAF Tucano awaiting take off at Belfast Harbour Airport (Short Brothers PLC).

Jaguar GR Mark 1A and T Mk 2A

In Service With:

6 Sqn	12 x Jaguar GR1A (1)	RAF Coltishall
	1 x Jaguar T2A	
54 Sqn	12 x Jaguar GR1A (2)	RAF Coltishall
	1 x Jaguar T2A (1)	
16 (R) Sqn	4 x Jaguar GR1A	RAF Lossiemouth
	4 x Jaguar T2A (2)	

Note: Figures in brackets refer to In Use Reserve (IUR) aircraft
Crew (GR 1A) 1 (T Mark 2A) 2; Length (GR 1A) 15.52m (T Mark 2A) 16.42m;
Wingspan 8.69m; Height 4.89m; All Up Operational Weight approx 11,000kgs;
Max Speed 1,350 km/ph(1056mph) Armament (GR 1A) 2 x 30mm Aden Cannon
(T Mark 2A) 1 x 30mm Aden Cannon, Martel, Sea Eagle, BL 755, bombs and
rockets; Engines 2 x Rolls-Royce Turbomeca Adour Mk 104s.

The Anglo-French Jaguar entered RAF service in 1973, the first aircraft being
delivered to the Operational Conversion Unit at RAF Lossiemouth in Scotland.
Powered by two Rolls Royce/Turbomeca Ardour turbofan engines, the Jaguar
was built by the BAC/Breguet consortium Sepecat. Two RAF versions remain in
service the GR1A and the T2A.

The Jaguar caries an impressive weapons load beneath four wing pylons and a
centre line pylon. Weapons include cluster bombs, 1,000 pound retarded and free
fall bombs and other bombs, rockets and missiles. The aircraft carries 30mm
cannon internally and for self defence the GR1A has a comprehensive suite of
electronic countermeasures, a radar warning receiver and overwing Sidewinder
missiles.

The most impressive feature of the Jaguar is the highly advanced and automated navigation and attack system. The "chisel" nose contains the Laser Ranging and Marked Target Seeker and, in addition to the on-board computer, there is a moving map display and a head-up display. The pilot can feed the data for his mission into the computer and all of the relevant information required for pin-point attack is supplied on the head-up display, showing him where the target is located and where to release the particular weapons being carried.

During the Gulf War, the RAF deployed a Squadron of 12 x Jaguar GR1A to the region. This squadron was employed on a variety of battlefield interdiction (BAI) and close air support (CAS) missions. Although only operating during daylight, the Jaguars displayed great versatility and flew over 600 operational sorties without loss. In addition to their operations over land, the Jaguars were also successful in destroying Iraqi patrol boats and landing craft in the Gulf. Jaguars also flew tactical reconnaissance sorties. Tornado GR1 and Jaguar GR1A's dropped some 100 x JP233 airfild denial weapons, 5000 x 1000 pound bombs 1,000 x LGBs, 100x ALARM mssiles and 700 x Air to Ground Rockets onto Iraqi positions.

Current MoD plans assume that the Jaguar will start to withdraw from service during 2004. Expect a Jaguar GR1A Squadron to have 16 established crews.

Harrier

In Service With:

1 Sqn	13 x Harrier GR7/T10	RAF Wittering
3 Sqn	13 x Harrier GR7/T10	RAF Laarbruch (closure 99)
4 Sqn	13 x Harrier GR7/T10	RAF Laarbruch (closure 99)
20 (R) Sqn	9 x Harrier GR7 (2)	RAF Wittering
	6 x Harrier T10 (1)	

Note: Figures in brackets refer to In Use Reserve (IUR) aircraft.

Crew (GR7) 1; (T Mark 10) 2; Length (GR7) 14m; Length (T10) 17m; Wingspan (normal) 9.3m; Height (GR7) 3.45m; Height (T10) 4.17m; Max Speed 1083 km/ph (673mph) at sea level; All Up Operational Weight approx 13,494kgs; Armament 2 x 30mm Aden guns, 4 x wing weapon pylons and 1 x underfuselage weapon pylon, conventional or cluster bombs; Engine 1 x Rolls-Royce Pegasus 11-21; Ferry Range 5,382 kms (3,310 miles) with 4 x drop tanks.

Capable of taking off and landing vertically, theHarrier is not tied to airfields with long concrete runways but can be dispersed to sites in the field close to the forward edge of the battle area. The normal method of operation calls for a short take off and vertical landing (STOVL), as a short ground roll on take off enables a greater weapon load to be carried. The Harrier GR3 was the mark of the aircraft that was taken into service in large numbers starting in 1969.

The Harrer GR5 entered servce in 1988 with the intention of replacing all of the RAF's GR3's on a one for one basis. However, the GR5 has been upgraded to the GR7, which in turn entered service in June 1990. All three of the operational Harrier squadrons have been equipped with the GR7 and all of the GR3s and GR5s have either been upgraded or withdrawn from service.

The differences in the GR5 and the GR7 are mainly in the avionics. The GR7 is equipped with the Forward Looking Infra Red (FLIR) equipment which, when combined with the night vision goggles (NVGs) that the pilot will wear, gives the GR7 a night, low level, poor weather capability. There are small differences in the cockpit layout of the two aircraft including layout and internal lighting standards. In most other respects, the GR7 is similar to the GR5.

The GR5/7 offers many advantages over the GR3. It posesses the capability to carry approoximately twice the weapon load over the same radius of action, or the same weapon load over over a much increased radius. In addition it carries a comprehensive ECM (Electronic Counter Measures) suite which can operate in the passive or active mode and will greatly enhance the GR5/7s chances of survival in today's high threat environment. The GR5/7 also has an inertial navigation system that is significantly more effective than that of the GR3.

The cockpit of the GR5/7 has been completely revised. The raising of the cockpit in relation to the aircraft has vastly improved the pilot's lookout. Furthermore, the design has incorporated the principle of Hands-On-Throttle and Stick (HOTAS). To aid systems management Cathode Ray Tube (CRT) displays are much in evidence for the display of the FLIR image, moving map, systems status and flying instruments displays. Each CRT has numerous multi-function reprogrammable keys for each function selection, again aiding systems management.

The LRMTS of the GR3 has been replaced with the Angle Rate Bombing System (ARBS) as the primary weapon aiming system. The ARBS incorporates a Dual MoDe Tracker, either TV colour contrasts or laser spot tracker. The GR5/7 has an increased wing area, improved aerodynamic qualities and the incorporation of Leading Edge Root Extensions which all combine to give the GR5/7 much improved manouvrability over that of the GR3. However, the GR5/7 maintains its ability to vector the engine's thrust in forward flight (VIFF), again increasing manouvrability.

The GR5/7 was derived from the McDonnell Douglas/British Aerospace AV-8B Noteworthy changes include the addition of a moving map display, Martin Baker ejection seat, increased bird strike protection, a new Aden 25mm cannon and additional electronic countermeasures equipment.

The T10 is an advanced trainer version of the aircraft. A total of 13 x Harrier T10 are on order with 9 in service by mid 1995. Deliveries should be complete during early 1996.

Expect a Harrier GR Squadron to have 17 established crews.

Nimrod

In Service With:

Maritime Reconnaissance

120 Sqn	7 x Nimrod MR2P (1)	RAF Kinloss
201 Sqn	7 x Nimrod MR2P (1)	RAF Kinloss
206 Sqn	7 x Nimrod MR2P	RAF Kinloss
42 (R) Sqn	3 x Nimrod MR2P	RAF Kinloss

Note: This group of units is known as the Kinloss Air Wing. We are reasonably certain that there are approximately 26 aircraft in this group at any one time. Aircraft are shown as being allocated to squadrons for ease of accounting - real numbers may change almost daily.

Figures in brackets refer to In Use Reserve (IUR) aircraft

Electronic Warfare

51 Sqn	3 Nimrod R1	RAF Wyton (Waddington 1995)

Characteristics MR2P:

Crew 12; Length 38.60m; Span 35m; Height 9.08m; Max Speed 926km ((575mph); Max All Up Weight 87,090 kgs; Endurance 12 hrs; Ferry Range 9265 kms; Armament Harpoon, Sidewinder, Sea Eagle, 9 x Mark 46 or Stingray Torpedoes, bombs; Engines 4 x Rolls Royce Spey RB 168-20 Mark 250 Turbofans.

There are currently two variants of the Nimrod in RAF service. The first is the

MR Mark 2P, which has been developed for long range maritime patrol. Its long ferry range enables the crew to moniter seaspace far to the north of Iceland and up to 4,000 kms out into the Western Atlantic. With AAR (Air to Air Refueling), its range and endurance is greatly extended. The MR Mark 2 is a very lethal submarine killer which carries the most up to date sensors and data procesing equipment linked to the weapon systems. In addition to weapons and sonarbouys, a searchlight mounted in the starboard wing pod can be used for search and rescue (SAR) operations.

The second version is the R Mark 1 which is specially fitted out for the gathering of electronic intelligence and only three are known to be in service. This is a highly secret aircraft that has been in RAF service since 1971 and about which little is known except that it has been spotted on patrol over the Baltic Sea.

Nimrod is a development of the basic Comet No 4C airframe which dates from the late 1940's. Both the current variants are descended from the original Nimrod MR Mark 1 version (first flight May 1967) that is no longer in service. Nimrod is a outstanding maritime patrol system and we are sure that, given the correct technical enhancements at frequent intervals, the aircraft will remain in service past the turn of the century.

The recently issued (1993) Staff Requirement (Air) 420, the "Replacement Maritime Patrol Aircraft" due in service in 1999, outlines a requirement for an aircraft with long endurance, anti-submarine capability, very long range (over the horizon) targeting and a search and rescue capability. Some possible airframe types to fit this requirement could range from civilian conversions of the Airbus or Boeing airliners, Atlantique 2, P-3 Orion, a maritime version of the FLA or a straight Nimrod upgrade.

Sentry AEW1

In Service With:

8 Sqn   6 x Sentry AEW1 (1)   RAF Waddington

Note: Figures in brackets refer to In Use Reserve (IUR) aircraft

186

Crew; 5 x Flight Crew and 12 x Mission Crew; Length 46.61m; Wingspan 44.42m; Height 12.73m; All Up Operational Weight 147,400kgs; Max Speed 853 km/ph (530 mph); Patrol Endurance 6 hours (can be enhanced by AAR); (Ferry Range 3,200 kms; Engines 4 x CFM-56-2A-3 ; Armament provision for self-defence air-to-air missiles.

Deliveries of the Sentry AEW1, commenced in March 1991 and delivery of all seven airframes was complete in early 1992. These seven aircraft are of the same type as the 18 delivered to the multi-national NATO early warning force between 1982/1985. All are equipped with the Joint Tactical Information Distribution System (JTIDS) and a 665,360 word memory secure communication system.
Powered by four CFM 56-2A-3 engines, the Sentry is designed to cruise at 29,000 feet whilst detecting air and surface contacts with its AN/APY-2 surveillance radar. Information is then transmitted back to interceptor aircraft and, ground, air and ship based units using a wide variety of digital data links.

Almost certainly the most complex airborne system yet to enter RAF service, the Sentry carries a crew of 17 which includes 5 x flight deck crew, 9 x mission crew and 3 x airborne technicians.

Hawk

In Service With:

100 Sqn	13 x Hawk T1/T1A (1)	RAF Finningley (closes 96)
4 FTS	20 x Hawk T1/T1A	RAF Valley
Red Arrows	10 x Hawk T1/T1A (1)	RAF Scampton (Cranwell 96)
Station Flight	2 x Hawk T1	RAF St Athan
Central Flying School	12 x Hawk T1/T1A	RAF Cranwell

Note: Figures in brackets refer to In Use Reserve (IUR) aircraft
Crew 2; Span 9.39m; Length 11.17m; Height 3.99m; Weight Empty 3647kg; Max Take Off Weight 8569kg; Max Speed 1038 kph (645 mph) at 3355m; Combat Radius 556 kms (345 miles); Engine 1 x 2359 kg thrust Rolls Royce/Turbomecca Adour Mk 151 turbofan; Armament 30mm Aden cannon, 2 x AIM-9L Sidewinder plus assorted bombs and rockets.

The Hawk first flew in 1974, and entered RAF service two years later both as an advanced flying trainer and a weapons training aircraft. It has an economical Adour engine - an un-reheated version of the same turbofan powering the Jaguar.

Hawks are used to teach operational tactics such as air to air and air to ground firing, air combat and low level operating procedures to pilots destined for the "fast-jet" squadrons. As a weapons trainer the Hawk is armed with an Aden cannon carried beneath the fuselage, and rocket pods or practice bombs can be fitted to underwing pylons. To fulfil its mobilisation role as a fighter aircraft, the Hawk carries a 30mm Aden cannon and two Sidewinder air-to-air missiles and is designated T1A. By 1995 about 50 Hawks will be equipped for the air defence mobilisation role.

The Hawk is a strong and rugged aircraft designed to cut training and maintenance costs. The aircraft has a long fatigue life to ensure a service career throughout the 1990s and beyond.

Eurofighter 2000

The Eurofighter 2000 (formerly EFA) is a highly agile, single seat, STOL capable aircraft optimised for air superiority/air defence and ground attack roles. The aircraft is part of a European co-production programme with the major manufacturing firms involved being British Aerospace, DASA, CASA and

Alenia. British Aerospace (BAe) is responsible for the front fuselage, foreplanes, starboard leading edge flaps and flaperons; BAe/CASA the starboard wing; Alenia the port wing; DASA the centre fuselage, fin and rudder; Alenia/CASA the rear fuselage.

Eurofighter is designed to carry 6 x medium range and 2 x close range air to air missiles. The aircraft has 13 x store stations and an internal one fitted on the starboard side. No Modifications will be necessary to carry "smart" weapons and 3 stations can carry external fuel pods. The Defensive Aids Sub-System (DASS) equipment is carried in 2 x wing pods that are an integral part of the wing. The aircraft will weigh about 37,000 lbs (approx 16,800 kgs) and be able to operate from a 500 metre strip.

The aircraft is designed to operate with a minimum of ground support requiring only 4 fitters to change an engine in 45 minutes, and a standard of nine man/servicing hours per flying hour as opposed to from 20 to 60 hours for other MoDern combat aircraft.

The first flight of the Eurofighter 2000 was made on April 15th 1994 from Manching Air base near Munich in Germany and when the aircraft arrives in service the current predictions are that the UK will have 250, Italy 110, Germany 140 and Spain 100. If everything goes to plan, the first aircraft should enter RAF service in the year 2000. The UK MoDs latest estimate is that some 300 British companies are in the Eurofighter supply chain, and that the project is currently supporting about 9,000 jobs. This figure is expected to rise to about 28,000 UK jobs during the peak production years.

C-130 Hercules

In Service With:

24 Sqn	12 x Hercules C1P/C3P/C1K (2)	RAF Lyneham
30 Sqn	12 x Hercules C1/C3/C1K (1)	RAF Lyneham
47 Sqn	12 x Hercules C1/C3 (1)	RAF Lyneham
70 Sqn	11 x Hercules C1/C3 (2)	RAF Lyneham
57 (R) Sqn	OCU 5 x Hercules	RAF Lyneham

Note: Figures in brackets refer to In Use Reserve (IUR) aircraft. The LTW appears to have a total of 54/55 aircraft. The squadron totals are given as a guide to what we believe are the average aircraft figures per squadron and the OCU at any one time.

Crew 5; Capacity 92 troops or 62 paratroops or 74 medical litters or 19,686kgs of freight; Length 29.78m; Span 40.41m; Height 11.66m; Weight Empty 34,287kgs; Max Load 45,093kgs; Max speed 618 km/ph (384mph); Service Ceiling 13,075m; Engines 4 x Allison T-56A-15 turboprops

The C-130 Herculs C1 is the workhorse of the RAF transport fleet. Over the years it has proved to be a versatile and rugged aircraft, primarily intended for tactical operations including troop carrying, paratrooping, supply dropping and aeromedical duties. The Hercules can operate from short unprepared airstrips, but also possesses the the endurance to mount long range strategic lifts if required. The aircraft is a derivative of the C-130E used by the United States Air Force, but is fitted with British Avionic equipment, a roller-conveyor system for heavy air-drops and with more powerful engines. The crew of five includes, pilot, co-pilot, navigator, air engineer and air loadmaster.

As a troop carrier, the Hercules can carry 92 fully armed men, while for airborne operations 62 paratroops can be dispatched in two simultaneous "sticks" through the fuselage side doors. Alternatively, 40 paratroops can jump from the rear loading ramp. As an air ambulance the aircraft can accommodate 74 stretchers.

Freight loads that can be parachuted from the aircraft include: 16 x 1 ton containers or 4 x 8,000 pound platforms or 2 x 16,000 pound platforms or 1 x platform of 30,000 pounds plus. Amongst the many combinations of military loads that can be carried in an air-landed operation are: 3 x Ferret scout cars plus 30 passengers or 2 x Land Rovers and 30 passengers or 2 x Gazelle helicopters.

Of the original 66 C1 aircraft, some 31 have been given a fuselage stretch poducing the Mark 3. The C3 "stretched version" provides an addtional 37% more cargo space. Refuelling probes have been fitted above the cockpit of both variants and some have received radar warning pods under the wing tips. One aircraft, designated Mark W2, is a special weather version and is located at the DERA Farnborough.

RAF Hercules are currently assisting in airlifting aid in support of UN operations in many areas of the world. For example, working from a forward airhead at Ancona on the eastern coast of Italy, a detachment of 38 officers and men with a single Hercules from 47 Sqn, averaged almost three flights a day for the year 3 July 1992 - 3 July 1993. Over 900 sorties lifted more than 19 million pounds of freight into Sarajevo. The aircraft were flown by six crews on a two week rotation from RAF Lyneham.

Current plans appear to be for the replacement of the RAF's ageing 1960s Hercules fleet during the next ten years and the UK MoD recently announced the purchase of 25 x C-130J from the US company Lockheed. This aircraft has improved engines, a new glass cockpit with flat screen displays and a two man crew. The first test and demonstrator aircraft are expected to be flying in September 1995 with production models available from the middle of 1996.

Orders for a second batch of 30 transport aircraft are believed to be in the system towards the end of the decade and the contenders will probably be Lockheed once again with a C-130 built to a new K standard and the FLA (future large aircraft). The FLA which will be built by the Rome based Euroflag Consortium, will probably be ready for service from about 2004 and could be capable of carrying a maximum payload of 30 tons as opposed to the 20 tons of the C-130J. British Aerospace is a member of Euroflag consortium.

The most commonly quoted argument in favour of the FLA is that this aircraft could carry a 25 ton payload over a distance of 4,000kms. Thus it is argued that a fleet of 40 x FLA could carry a UK Brigade to the Gulf within 11.5 days, as opposed to the 28.5 days required to make a similar deployment with 40 x C-130s.

Over 1,000 x C-130 have been manufactured and 467 are in service with the US Armed Forces.

Tucano

In Service With:

Central Flying School - RAF Cranwell
1 FTS - RAF Linton-on-Ouse
3 FTS - RAF Cranwell
6 FTS - RAF Finningley (closure 1996)

Crew 2; Length 9.86m; Height 3.40m; Span 11.14m; Max Speed 458 km/ph (254mph); Service Ceiling 8750m; Range 1916kms; Engine 1100shp Garrett 8TPE-331 turboprop.

Originally designed by the Brazilian aerospace company Embracer, the Tucano was selected in 1985 to replace the Jet Provost as the RAF's basic trainer.

The development and production contract was awarded to Shorts of Belfast, who have incorporated a number of Modifications to meet the RAF's specifications.

The first aircraft was delivered in June 1988 although two aircraft had been at Boscombe Down undergoing flight trials since late 1987. Student training on the aircraft started at RAF Church Fenton in December 1989.

The RAF version of the Tucano, designated the Tucano T1, has been Modified in many ways from the basic Embracer 312. A Garrett TOE 331 engine which develops 1,100 shp, is fitted in place of the original PT6 and represents a 50% power increase. Fatigue life has been extended from 8,000 to 12,000 hours by fitting strengthened wings and landing gear, a ventral air brake has been added, plus a new canopy which is bird strike resistant up to 270 knots.

The Tucano heralds a new concept of flying training within the RAF. The tandem seating, in Martin Baker ejector seats, allows a smaller aerodynamic frontal area than the Jet Provost, leading to lower power requirements and greater fuel efficiency. Visibility from the cockpit is also improved and the student is better prepared to progress to the Hawk advanced trainer.

The turbo-engine is both flexible and economic, helping the Tucano to out-perform the Jet Provost in every area except maximum straight-and-level speed. For example, the Tucano time to 15,000 feet is half of that required by the Jet Provost.

The Tucano has been manufactured around the concept of reliability and maintainbility to provide a cost-effective trainer and fulfil the requirements of the RAF through the 1990s and beyond. There are 126 Tucano in RAF service.

Chinook

In Service With:

7 Sqn	9 x Chinook HC2 (3)	RAF Odiham
	1 x Gazelle HT3	
18 Sqn	3 x Chinook HC2 (1)	RAF Laarbruch
	4 x Puma HC1(1)	
78 Sqn	1 x Chinook HC2 (1)	RAF MPA (Falklands)
	2 x Sea King HAR3	
27(R) Sqn	5 x Chinook HC2	RAF Odiham
	4 x Puma HC1(1)	

Note: Figures in brackets refer to In Use Reserve (IUR) aircraft. RAF Laarbruch closes in 1999.

Crew 3; Fuselage Length 15.54m; Width 3.78m; Height 5.68m; Weight (empty) 10,814kgs; Internal Payload 8,164kgs; Rotor Diameter 18.29m; Cruising Speed 270 km/ph (158mph); Service Ceiling 4,270m; Mission Radius(with internal and external load of 20,000kgs including fuel and crew) 55kms; Rear Loading Ramp Height 1.98m; Rear Loading Ramp Width 2.31m; Engines 2 x Avco Lycoming T55-L11E turboshafts.

The Chinook is a tandem-rotored, twin-engined medium lift helicopter. It has a crew of four (pilot, navigator and 2 x crewmen) and is capable of carrying 45 fully equipped troops or a variety of heavy loads up to approximately 10 tons. The first Chinooks entered service with the RAF in 1982. The triple hook system allows greater flexibility in load carrying and enables some loads to be carried faster and with greater stability. In the ferry configuration with internally mounted fuel tanks, the Chinook's range is over 1,600 kms (1,000 miles). In the medical evacuation role the aircraft can carry 24 stretchers.

RAF Chinook aircraft are currently being upgraded to the HC2 standard. The first of the 32 aircraft being upgraded was delivered to the RAF in the Spring of 1993, with the remaining aircraft due to be modified by the end of 1995. The HC2 upgrade, for which a total of £145 million has been allocated, allows for the aircraft to be modified to the US CH-47D standard with some extra enhancements. These enhancements include fitting infra-red jammers, missile approach warning indicators, chaff and flare dispensers, a long range fuel system and machine gun mountings.

This is a rugged and reliable aircraft. During the Falklands War reports suggest that, at one stage 80 fully equipped troops were carried in one lift and, during a Gulf War mission a single Chinook carried 110 Iraqi POWs. The Chinook mid-life update will significantly enhance the RAF's ability to support the land forces during the next 25 years.

Since 1 April 1990 the RAF Chinook fleet has flown some 44,200 hours during which time the operating costs (personnel, full and maintenance) have been £232 million, a figure that results in a cost of £5,248 per flying hour. On average 18 of the 32 aircraft have been available for front-line service at any one time a figure reflecting the need for planned maintenance and servicing. On 9 March 1995 the UK MoD announced a purchase of a further 14 x Chinooks and a separate buy of 22 x EH-101. The contract for the 14 x Chinooks was signed in early September 1995 at a price of £240 million (US$365) resulting in a possible unit cost of 17 million per aircraft

Puma

In Service With:

18 Sqn	4 x Puma HC1(1)	RAF Laarbruch
	3 x Chinook HC2 (1)	
33 Sqn	10 x Puma HC1(2)	RAF Odiham
230 Sqn	13 x Puma HC1(2)	RAF Aldergrove
27(R) Sqn	4 x Puma HC1(1)	RAF Odiham
	5 x Chinook HC2	

Note: Figures in brackets refer to In Use Reserve (IUR) aircraft. RAF Laarbruch closes in 1999.

Crew 2 or 3; Fuselage Length 14.06m; Width 3.50m; Height 4.38m; Weight (empty) 3,615kg; Maximum Take Off Weight 7,400kgs; Cruising Speed 258 km/ph (192mph); Service Ceiling 4,800m; Range 550kms; Engines 2 x Turbomecca Turmo 111C4 turbines.

The "package deal" between the UK and France on helicopter collaboration dates back to February 1967 when Ministers of the two countries signed a Memorandum of Understanding (MOU). The programme covered the development of three helicopter types - the Puma, Gazelle and Lynx. The main

contractors engaged on the programme were Westland and SNIAS for the airframe, and Rolls Royce and Turbomeca for the engines.

Development of the Puma was already well advanced in France when collaboration began. However, the flight control system has been developed jointly by the two countries, and a great deal of work done by Westland to adapt the helicopter for the particular operational requirements of the RAF. Production of the aircraft was shared between the two countries, the UK making about 20% by value of the airframe, slightly less for the engine as well as assembling the aircraft procured for the RAF. Deliveries of the RAF Pumas started in 1971.

The Puma is powered by 2 x Turbomeca Turmo 111C4 engines mounted side by side above the main cabin. Capable of many operational roles Puma can carry 16 fully equipped troops, or 20 at light scales. In the casualty evacuation role (CASEVAC), 6 stretchers and 6 sitting cases can be carried. Underslung loads of up to 3,200kgs can be transported over short distances and an infantry battalion can be moved using 34 Puma lifts.

Sea King HAR3

In Service With:

202 Sqn	7 x Sea King HAR3 (2)	RAF Lossiemouth/Boulmer and Leconfield
22 Sqn	5 x Sea King HAR3 (1) 2 x Wessex HC2	RAF Valley and Wattisham
78 Sqn	2 x Sea King HAR3 1 x Chinook HC2 (1)	RAF MPA

Note: Figures in brackets refer to In Use Reserve (IUR) aircraft.

Crew 1-3; Length 17.01m; Height 4.72m;Rotor Diameter 18.9m; Weight (empty) 6201kg; Cruising Speed 208 km/ph (129mph); Range 1230kms; Engine 2 x Rolls Royce Gnome H1400.1 turboshafts.

The Westland Sea King HAR3 Search and Rescue helicopter entered RAF service in 1978. The aircraft is powered by two Rolls Royce Gnome gas turbine engines, each rated at 1,660 shaft horse power and is fitted with advanced all-weather search and navigation equipment, as well as autopilot and onboard computer to assist positioning and hovering at night or in bad weather. In addition to four crew members the HAR3 can carry up to six stretchers, or 18 survivors. Under normal conditions expect the HAR3 to have an operational radius of approximately 448 kms (280 miles).

The Sea King HAR3 will replace the Wessex HC2 in the SAR role by 1996. A recent MoD report concluded that a total of 25 Sea Kings were required to ensure that SAR duties were carried out effectively and an announcement was made in mid 1992 of an order for 6 more HAR3, to bring the total up to the required 25. Of these 25 aircraft, 12 will be required for SAR duties in the UK, 2 in the Falkland Islands, 4 will be necessary for conversion training and the remaining 7 will form an engineering and operational pool.

RAF Weapons

Sidewinder AIM-9L
Diameter 0.127m: Span 0.63m: Length 2.85m: Total Weight 85.3kgs: Warhead Weight 10.2kg: Propulsion Solid fuel rocket: Speed Mach 2.5: Range 17.7kms.

The Sidewinder missile which is carried by all of the RAF's air defence aircraft, is an infra-red weapon which homes onto the heat emitted by a hostile aircraft's engines. Sidewinder can operate independently of the aircraft's radar, and provides the air defence aircraft with an alternative method of attacking targets at shorter ranges. Sidewinder has an excellent dogfight capability.

Sky Flash
Length 3.66m; Diameter 0.203m; Span 1.02m; Weight 192kgs; Warhead Weight 30kgs; Marconi monopulse semi - active radar homing system; Range 50kms

Sky Flash is an advanced radar guided air-to-air missile based on the Sparrow which was taken into service in 1977, but with improved guidance and fusing systems. Designed to operate in severe electronic counter-measure conditions, it has an all weather high/low altitude attack capability. Sky Flash is in service on the F3 air defence variant of the Tornado. It is currently the RAF's major air defence weapon.

Sea Eagle
Length 4.14m: Diameter 0.40m: Span 1.20m: Total Weight 590kg: Warhead Weight (not yet revealed) believed to be 200kg+: Speed Mach 0.9+: Range 50-100kms depending on launch altitude: Propulsion 1 x Microturbo TRI -l-60-1 turbojet delivering 367kg of thrust.

The Sea Eagle, a long range anti-ship guided missile, is used by the Tornado GR1 and Nimrod in the maritime attack role. Developed from the Martel, Sea Eagle can attack targets over the horizon at very low level using radar guidance and an on-board microprocessor which stores the target's last known position and speed. Powered by a small air-breathing-turbojet, the missile skims the waves at just under the speed of sound and picks up the target with its very advanced active radar seeker.

ALARM
Length 4.24m: Diameter 0.22m: Span 0.72m: Total Weight 175kg: Propellant 1 x Royal Ordnance Nuthatch solid fuel two stage rocket: Range and speed not yet revealed, however these figures are probably comparable with those of HARM which has a speed of Mach 3+ and a range of 75kms+.

ALARM stands for Air Launched Anti-Radiation Missile and this type has recently been introduced into RAF Service. The missile is launched at low level near the suspected site of an enemy radar and after launch rapidly climbs to about 12,000m. At this height, a small parachute opens and the missile descends earthwards while the on-board radar searches the broad band for emissions from enemy radar. Once a target has been identified, the motor is re-ignited and the missile makes a supersonic dive onto the target.

The total RAF buy in the first manufacturing run was believed to be some 750 missiles.

ASRAAM

The ASRAAM (Advanced Short Range Air to Air Missile) fire-and-forget missile, is an air combat weapon that is highly manoeuvrable and requires minimal pilot input. The missile has an advanced high sensitivity infra-red seeker, which can lock onto the target before launch or in flight, and results in an extremely high kill probability. ASRAAM is also highly resistant to electronic countermeasures. We believe that the current planned RAF in service date (ISD) for the missile is 1998.

AMRAAM

Length 3.6 metres; weight 340 lbs; cruising speed Mach 4; range approx 30 miles

AMRAAM (Advanced medium range air-to-air missile)is an air fighting weapon that matches the fire-and-forget capability of the ASRAAM, but with greater range. There is increased immunity over electronic countermeasures and a low-smoke, high impulse rocket motor to reduce the probability of an enemy sighting the missile. Present plans for the RAF are unclear. However, AMRAAM will be in service with the Fleet Air Arm from 1995 and the initial purchase is believed to be about 210 missiles.

BL 755 Cluster Bomb

Length 2.45m: Diameter .41m: Weight 277kg: Payload 147 bomblets.

The BL 755 is a system which was designed to cope with some of the very large area targets that might be encountered on the Central Front, especially large Warsaw Pact armoured formations of Regimental strength (90+ tanks) or more. The weapon can be carried by Tornado GR1, Harrier, Jaguar, Buccaneer and Phantom and consists of a large container which is divided into seven compartments. Each of these compartments contains 21 bomblets making a total of 147 bomblets in all.

After the bomb has been released from the aircraft, the 147 bomblets are ejected and fall to the ground covering a wide area. As each individual bomblet hits a target, a HEAT charge is detonated which can fire a large slug of molten metal through up to 250mm of armour. In addition, the casing of the bomblet disintegrates and hundreds of fragments of shrapnel are dispersed over a wide area, with resultant damage to personnel and soft skinned vehicles.

The BL 755 can be released at very low altitude and this is essential if pilots are to survive in the high density SAM conditions that will apply over the modern battlefield. Aircraft will only have the chance to make one pass over the target before the defences are alerted, and for a pilot to make a second pass to ensure accuracy would be suicidal.

JP 233 Airfield Attack System
Designed for use by the Tornado GR1, the JP 233 has recently entered RAF service. A Tornado will carry two JP 233 systems and each system is comprised of a dispenser which releases 30 cratering sub-munitions and 215 area denial sub-munitions (mines) over a wide area. The cratering sub-munitions penetrate the runway and explode leaving large holes which render its use by aircraft impossible. The area denial sub-munitions rest on the surface in the vicinity of the craters and make repair work very dangerous until cleared by specialist teams.

JP 233 has a variety of uses against a whole range of targets besides airfields

THAAD
Recent fears of nuclear proliferation, and the problems of nuclear capable delivery systems such as the former Soviet Scud missile being used by nations who hitherto have not been able to mount a credible threat to the UK, have forced the MoD to look at the options offered by adopting a high level missile defence.

We believe that the UK MoD is now looking at a Theatre High-Altitude Area Defence (THAAD) system for defending the UK against incoming missiles. The MoD appears to be interested in creating a layered anti-missile defence, capable of multiple attempts at hitting targets at ranges of over 100 miles and at heights of over 100,000 feet, to shorter range systems such as the US Patriot that could hit targets at much closer range.

During late 1993, officials from the US Lockheed Corporation briefed UK MoD staff on the capabilities of THAAD and in November 1993, more than 60 companies attended a presentation regarding work on such a system. However, we believe that the UK can only proceed in such an expensive programme, as a partner in a European collaborative project, and there are some reports that preliminary talks have taken place to explore options.

A layered system based upon low, medium and high level missiles, employing satellite and early warning aircraft detectors would have a very high percentage chance of success against everything except a saturation attack by large numbers of missiles. However, the defence budgets of the nations that really count in the European procurement scene (France, Germany and the UK) appear to be fully committed until at least 2005. An expensive THAAD system, costing many billions of pounds is almost certainly not going to appear in the short term.

In February 1994, the UK Secretary of State for Defence announced that a £3.5 million study into ballistic missile defences would take place

RAF Regiment

The need to raise a dedicated specialist force to protect air installations became apparent during WWII when unprotected aircraft on the ground were vulnerable to enemy air and ground attack. Consequently, the RAF Regiment was raised on 1 February 1942 by a Royal Warrant of King George VI. At the end of WWII, there were over 85,000 personnel serving in the RAF Regiment manning 240 operational squadrons. During late 1993, the strength of the RAF Regiment was approximately 3,000 (including 264 officers). Following restructuring, strength is believed to be planned at about 2,400 by mid 1995.

Currently the RAF Regiment exists to provide ground and short range air defence for RAF installations, and to train all of the RAF's combatant personnel to enable them to contribute to the defence of their units.

As of 1 January 1996 RAF Regiment units are as follows:

No 1 Group (STC)

No 2 Squadron	Honnington	Field Squadron
No 3 Squadron	Aldergrove	Field Squadron

No 2 Group (STC)

No 1 Squadron	Laarbruch	Field Squadron
No 26 Squadron	Laarbruch	Rapier
No 37 Squadron	Bruggen	Rapier

No 11 Group (STC)

No 15 Squadron	Leeming	Rapier
No 27 Squadron	Leuchars	Rapier
No 48 Squadron	Lossiemouth	Rapier

British Forces Cyprus (STC)

No 34 Squadron	Akrotiri	Field Squadron

Independent STC Units

No 63 (QCS)	Uxbridge	Ceremonial/Field Squadron

PTC Units

RAF Regiment Depot	Honnington
Rapier Training Unit	Honnington

Specialist RAF Regiment training for gunners is given at the RAF Regiment Depot at Honnington. On completion of training at the RAF College Cranwell officers also undergo further specialist training at RAF Honnington, and in some cases the School of Infantry at Warminster in Wiltshire or the Royal School of Artillery at Larkhill. The RAF Regiment also mans the Queen's Colour Squadron which undertakes all major ceremonial duties for the Royal Air Force.. These duties involve mounting the Guard at Buckingham Palace on an occasional basis, and providing Guards of Honour for visiting Heads of State. The Queen's Colour Squadron also has a war role as a field squadron.

The regiment is not alone in defending any RAF station. Every airman based at a station has a ground defence role and is trained to defend his place of work against ground attack and attack by NBC weapons. Training for this is given by RAF Regiment instructors who provide courses at station level on various aspects of ground defence for all personnel.

There are now two basic RAF Regiment squadron organisations - the Field Squadron organised for ground defence against possible enemy ground action and the Rapier Squaron organised for defence against low-flying enemy aircraft. There are four dedicated field squadrons and 63 (QCS) Squadron with a dual ceremonial/field squadron role. Five rapier squadrons defend RAF airbases.

Rapier Squadron-Possible Organisation

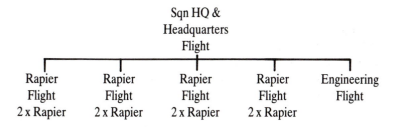

Rapier Characteristics - Guidance Semi Automatic to Command Line of Sight (SACLOS); Missile Diameter 13.3 cm; Missile Length 2.35m; Rocket Solid Fuelled; Warhead High Explosive; Launch Weight 42kg; Speed Mach 2+; Ceiling 3,000m; Maximum Range 6,800m; Fire Unit Height 2.13m; Fire Unit Weight 1,227kg; Radar Height (in action) 3.37m; Radar Weight 1,186kg; Optical Tracker Height 1.54m; Optical Tracker Weight 119kg; Generator Weight 243kg; Generator Height 0.91m

The Rapier system provides area, Low Level Air Defence (LLAD) over the area around the airbase to be defended. It consists of an Optical Tracker, a Fire Unit, a Radar and a Generator. The into-action time of the system is thought to be about 15 minutes and the radar is believed to scan out to 12km. Each fire unit can therefore cover an Air Defence Area (ADA) of about 100 square kms. Having discharged the 4 missiles on a Fire Unit, 2 men are thought to be able to carry out a reload in about 3 minutes. During the Falklands Campaign, Rapier was credited with 14 kills and 6 probables from a total of 24 missiles fired.

We believe that Rapier in service with the RAF Regiment are Field Standard B1(M) and that these equipments will be ugraded to Field Standard C (Rapier 2000).

Rapier FSC will offer significant enhancements to performance. The towed system launcher will mount eight missiles (able to fire two simultaneously at 2 separate targets) which will be manufactured in two warhead versions. One of these warheads will be armour piercing to deal with fixed wing targets, and the other a fragmentation warhead for the engagement of cruise missiles and RPVs. Rapier 2000 will have the Darkfire tracker and a tailor made 3-dimensional radar system for target acquisition developed by Plessey.

A Joint Service Rapier FSC OCU has formed at RAF Honnington to oversee both the RAF's and Army's conversion to the new system. No 48 Sqn at RAF Lossiemouth is planned to be the first unit to convert to Rapier FSC in 1994 and the final squadron conversion should take place in 1995.

Rapier has now been sold to the armed forces of at least 14 nations. We believe that sales have amounted to over 25,000 missiles, 600 launchers and 350 Blindfire radars.

During June 1993 the UK MoD announced a reorganisation of the reserve forces and that by 1997, about 50% of the complement of No 15 Squadron (RAF Leeming) and No 27 Squadron (RAF Leuchars), both equipped with Rapier, would be members of the Royal Auxiliary Air Force Regiment.

Royal Auxiliary Air Force Regiment (RAuxAF Regt)

Airfield defence is further enhanced by squadrons of the RAuxAF Regt who are recruited locally and whose role is the ground defence of the airfield and its associated outlying installations. A RAuxAF Regt Sqn has an all up strength of about 120 men and costs approximately £500,000 a year to keep in service. As a general rule, a squadron has a headquarters flight, two mobile flights mounted in

Land Rovers and two flights for static guard duties. RAuxAF Regt squadrons are as follows:

1310 Wing RAuxAF Regt	RAF Honnington	HQ Unit
2503 Sqn RAuxAF Regt	RAF Waddington	Ground Defence
2620 Sqn RAuxAF Regt	RAF Marham	Ground Defence
2622 Sqn RAuxAF Regt	RAF Lossiemouth	Ground Defence
2624 Sqn RAuxAF Regt	RAF Brize Norton	Ground Defence
2625 Sqn RAuxAF Regt	RAF St Mawgan	Ground Defence

RAF Reserves

The reserve component of the Royal Air Force in early 1994 was as follows:

RAuxAF & RAFVR Reserves	-	2,200
Reserve Officers	-	600
Class E Airmen/Airwomen	-	11,000
Airmen Pensioners	-	22,000
Officer Pensioners	-	8,000
Total		43,800

* Aircrew who have served on Short Service Commissions have a mandatory reserve liability of four years.

The Controller Reserve Forces (RAF) is located at RAF Innsworth as part of RAF PTC. He is responsible for all of the non operational aspects of reserve forces policy and co-ordination, ranging from recruitment, through training, promotions and welfare to future planning. The following are the formed Reserve Units (RAuxAF Regt Squadrons are listed in the preceeding RAF Regiment section).

Royal Auxiliary Air Force

No 1 Maritime HQ	Northwood (London)
No 2 Maritime HQ	Pitrivie (Scotland)
No 3 Maritime HQ	RAF St Mawgan
4624 Movements Sqn	RAF Brize Norton Air Movements
4626 Aeromedical Evacuation Sqn	RAF Hullavington

Royal Auxiliary Air Force Defence Force Flights

RAuxAF Defence Force Flight (Brampton)
RAuxAF Defence Force Flight (High Wycombe)
RAuxAF Defence Force Flight (Lyneham)
RAuxAF Defence Force Flight (St Athan)

Royal Air Force Volunteer Reserve

7000 Flight, Royal Air Force Volunteer Reserve
7010 Flight, Royal Air Force Volunteer Reserve
7630 Flight, Royal Air Force Volunteer Reserve
7644 Flight, Royal Air Force Volunteer Reserve

In war, these four flights would provide specialist assistance in public relations, foreign language interrogation, photographic interpretation and intelligence support.

Note: There are currently believed to be approximately 2,000 posts with the RAuxAF and a further 200 with the RAFVR. Proposals have been announced by the MoD for both of these organisations to be amalgamated, producing a more streamlined organisation for war.

PART 5 - THE CIVILIAN SECTOR

The MoD's Civilian Staff

The three uniformed services are supported by the civilian staff of the Ministry of Defence. On the 1st April 1995 some 116,139 permanent UK based civilian personnel were working in the following three main areas:

MoD Operational Areas	26,597
Military Support Areas	54,728
HQ, Procurement Executive & Support Functions	34,814

In a clear and unambiguous statement in 1994, the UK MoD stated that "The Department remains committed to a process of civilianisation. Increasingly, it makes no sense to employ expensively trained and highly professional military personnel in jobs which civilians could do equally well. Civilians are generally cheaper than their military counterparts and as they often remain longer in post can provide greater continuity. For these reasons, it is our long-standing policy to civilianise posts and so release valuable military resources to the front line whenever it makes operational and economic sense to do so".

In addition to the permanent UK based civilians there were approximately 16,600 locally entered civilian personnel distributed around the following locations:

Continental Europe *	11,903
Gibraltar	1,302
Malta	8
Cyprus	2,250
Hong Kong	666
Brunei	182
Nepal	293
Elsewhere	35

Note * - The overwhelming majority of this figure are locally entered civilians supporting BFG (British Forces Germany).

In general terms the permanent UK based civilian personnel are allocated to the TLBH (Top Level Budget Holders) as follows:

Royal Naval Operational Areas	4,500
Army Operational Areas	16,800
RAF Operational Areas	4,600
Overseas Garrisons	7,000
Naval Home Command	3,700
Adjutant General	8,100
RAF Personnel & Training Command	4,200
Chief of Fleet Support	18,900
Quartermaster General	11,700
RAF Logistics Command	8,200
MoD HQ & Centrally Managed Expenditure	14,900
Procurement Executive	6,200
Other Areas (Including DERA)	13,600

Since 1979 there has been a dramatic fall in the numbers of both permanent UK and locally entered civilian staff. In 1979 the combined figures were just under 300,000 personnel; and by 1995 this figure had fallen to a combined total of just over 130,000.

In general the MoD Civil Servants work in a parallel stream with their respective uniformed counterparts. There are some "stand alone" civilian agencies of which the DERA is probably the largest.

The Defence Evaluation & Research Agency (Dera)

From 1st April 1995 a new organisation, the Defence Evaluation & Research Agency (DERA) has assumed the responsibilities of its predecessor the Defence Research Agency (DRA). This new organisation combines the activities of a number of research and evaluation agencies under the umbrella of a new top level budget holder. Agencies such as the Directorate General of Test and Evaluation, the Chemical and Biological Defence Establishment and the Defence Operational Analysis Centre have been grouped together in the new agency with a staff strength of some 12,000 people and an operational budget of just over 500 million.

The DERA is organised into four major operational divisions:

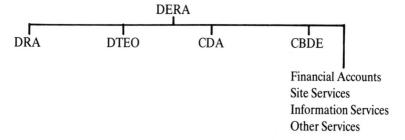

DRA Division - Includes all except two of the old DRA's scientific business operations.

DTEO - The Defence Test and Evaluation Organisation consists of the Director General of Tests and Evaluation plus some other smaller elements operating in the DTEO sector from the from the old DRA.

CBDE - This division combines the activities of the old Chemical and Biological Defence Establishment at Porton Down in Wiltshire with the old DRA's Chemical and Electronics department.

CDA - Centre for Defence analysis combines the activities of the old Defence Operational Analysis Centre and the DRAs Operational Studies Department

The current priorities of the DERA as described by the UK MoD are:
a. To keep the armed forces well equipped with modern capable equipment.
b. To support mobile and flexible response forces.
c. Support the procurement of military equipment which is sustainable, has high reliability and availability, and gives good value for money.
d. Ensure that the research programme reflects the changing international situation and defence objectives.
e. Maintain the longer-term research programme to sustain the science and technology base.

f. Place greater emphasis on research programmes aimed at reducing through life costs.

g. Encourage the greatest possible industrial participation in maintaining the technological base; and exploit academic expertise.

DERA Budget 1995-1996	- £506.3 million
DERA Personnel Figures (at 1 April 1995)	- 8,900 non Industrial
	- 2,500 Industrial

The United Kingdom Defence Industry

Despite the demise of the Warsaw Pact, uncertainties over our future defence strategy and substantial cuts in defence spending, the United Kingdom's Defence Industry has proved to be a remarkably resilient and successful element of our national manufacturing base. In the early 1990's defence related production accounted for some 11% of manufactured output in the United Kingdom. Coincidentally, defence work also provided employment for just under 10% of our manufacturing workforce employing 410,000 individuals in 1991. Despite the rationalisation which is still taking place within the defence sector, it is generally accepted that defence employment still puts around £6 billion annually into the broader UK economy via salaries paid throughout the supply chain.

Historically, the UK defence industry has possessed the capability and competence to provide a wide range of advanced equipments to support our own Armed Forces. This capability, matched with their competitiveness, has enabled UK companies to command a sizeable share of those overseas markets for which export licence approvals are available. At home, UK industry has consistently provided some 75% by value of the equipment requirements of The Ministry of Defence. In simple terms, in recent years the industry has supplied £9 - 10 billion worth of goods and services for our Armed Forces annually while a further £3 - 5 billion worth of business has accrued to the UK defence industry from sales to approved overseas customers. The spread of overheads resulting from export sales has also benefitted The Ministry of Defence to the extent of some £350 million per annum.

The United Kingdom's defence companies are justifiably proud of their record in recent years in the face of fierce overseas competition.

Reductions in our Armed Forces and the heavy demands on our remaining Service personnel, who face an unpredictable international security environment, make it inevitable that considerable reliance will be placed upon the support and surge capacity offered by our comprehensive indigenous defence industrial base. Without this effective industrial base, the ability of UK to exert independence of action or influence over collective security arrangements would be constrained. It is essential that government policies ensure that industry retains the necessary capabilities to support our forces in a changing world.

Up until now the United Kingdom's defence industry has been highly successful in supporting the United Kingdom's Armed Forces with high quality equipment and it has also made a significant contribution to our balance of payments. As a strategic resource it is vitally important that it should attract the appropriate levels of research and development funding to maintain the necessary technical excellence and production facilities to meet the needs of the future.

As importantly, the defence industry is not only a major employer but it is also the generator of high technology that is readily adaptable to civilian use in fields such as avionics and engine technology. The future of the UK's defence industry will almost certainly have to be properly planned if it is to remain an efficient and essential national support organisation in times of crisis. A look at MoD payments to contractors during 1994-95 identifies some of the larger manufacturers.

Major Contractors Listing

Contractors Paid More Than £250 Million During 1994-95
British Aerospace plc (BAe)
General Electric Co plc (GEC)
Hunting plc
Rolls Royce plc
VSEL plc
Building and Property Facilities Management Ltd

Companies Paid Between £100 Million and £250 Million During 1994-95

Babcock International Group plc
British Telecommunications plc
Devonport Management plc
ICI plc
John Mowlem & Co plc
LORAL ASIC
Serco Group plc
Siemens plc
Vickers plc
Westland Group plc

Companies Paid Beween £50 Million and £100 Million During 1994-95

Amec plc
BICC plc
British Petroleum Co plc
Civil Aviation Authority
ESSO UK plc
General Motors Corporation
MMS Space Systems Ltd
Sema Group plc
Thorn EMI plc
Trafalgar House plc
WS Atkins Ltd

At the time of writing the four primary UK defence companies are BAe, GEC, Hunting and Rolls Royce (GEC having recently acquired VSEL). Brief Outlines of these companies are as follows

GEC (The General Electric Company)

GEC is organised into a number of major divisions of which the Electronic Systems Division is the major player in the defence manufacturing sector
These divisions are as follows:

Electronic Systems
Consumer Goods

Medical Equipment
Power Systems
Electronic Metrology
Electronic Components
Telecommunications
Office Equipment & Printing
Industrial Apparatus
Distribution & Trading

The total group turnover during the 1995 Financial Year was £10,330 million with an operating profit of £714 million. During this period there was an average total worldwide number of employees of just over 82,000, of whom over 56,000 were working in the United Kingdom

GEC Electronic Systems

The Electronic System Group undertakes the great majority of GEC's defence business. It also produces systems with civilian applications, particularly in communications and avionics. These account for some 25 per cent of annual sales.

Turnover (1995)   £2,662 million
Profit   £205 million

In the UK and in some overseas countries the Group trades under the "GEC-Marconi" name. GEC-Marconi is one of Europe's largest defence electronics suppliers whose product range includes avionic systems, underwater weapons and sonars, all types of radars, terrestrial and satellite communications, guided missiles, warships, electronic warfare systems and data transmission systems. Business is conducted on a worldwide basis with major sales in Europe, North America, the Middle East and the Far East. Many international collaborations and partnerships are involved. For example, the company is a major contributor to the European Fighter Aircraft and the company has merged its space activities with the French company Matra to form Matra Marconi Space, a world leader in the space business.

213

The group spends several hundred million pounds annually on research and development to enhance and update its considerable technology base and has three research laboratories specialising in technologies as diverse as integrated microwave circuits, infrared materials, signal processing and liquid crystal displays.

This technology base has been put to good use in the development of products for non-defence applications. Some notable examples include fly-by-wire systems for civil airliners, including the systems chosen for the Boeing 777, in-flight video entertainment systems for air passengers, a low-cost videophone which can operate worldwide over standard analogue telephone lines and receivers for satellite TV systems already installed in several million homes.

The Electronic Systems Group has major businesses in Canada, the US, France, Italy and Australia and has offices or representational arrangements in most major countries in the world.

During 1994-95 GEC-Marconi Defence Systems won further orders for TIALD laser designator pods; the pod has been successfully integrated into the Jaguar aircraft. GEC-Marconi's naval systems business (torpedoes, sonars, combat systems and warships) had a successful year with a major order for the production of Spearfish torpedoes secured, together with further export orders for Tigerfish torpedoes.

Yarrow Shipbuilders (a GEC Subsidiary) is the UK lead contractor for the Common New Generation Frigate, a UK, French and Italian collaborative programme; an international joint venture company has been formed to undertake the design. The acquisition of Ferranti Naval Systems has strengthened the scope of the Group in naval command systems.

A substantial order for the design and initial production for an off-board countermeasures decoy has been received from the Royal Navy. Another subsidiary, GEC-Marconi Dynamics has continued to make progress on its major programmes for guided missiles. In addition to homing heads, it supplied precision guided munitions with a wide range of payloads to match different types of target.

Additional orders were won by Marconi Command and Control Systems for gun control equipment and simulators fo the British Army's Challenger 2 main battle tank. The Marksman anti-aircraft gun turret performed successfully in customer trials.

VSEL & GEC

During early 1995 GEC concluded its bid for submarine maker Vickers Shipbuilding & Engineering Limited (VSEL PLC), when its offer was accepted by the VSEL shareholders.

As the UK's largest warship builder, VSEL, sited at Barrow-in-Furness in Cumbria, is a shipyard of great strategic importance. Today, it is the only UK designer and manufacturer of nuclear and conventionally powered submarines, with a capability for large surface warships.

The acquisition of VSEL is significant for GEC. With its frigate building yard at Yarrow Shipbuilders in Glasgow, and its combat systems, defence systems, underwater weapons and sonar systems divisions, GEC now has a totally integrated naval systems capability. Together with its proven strength in systems integration, GEC is a world class supplier of warships and naval systems.

Electronic Systems Subsidiaries & Associated Companies
GEC-Marconi Ltd
    Combat Systems
    Sonar Systems
    Ferranti-Thomson Sonar
    Systems UK Ltd (50.0%)
    Underwater Weapons
Yarrow Shipbuilders Ltd
GEC-Marconi Radar & Defence Systems
    GEC-Marconi Defence Systems
    Navigation & Electro-Optics
    GEC-Marconi Secure Systems Ltd
    GEC-Marconi Dynamics Ltd
Marconi Dynamics Inc, USA

Marconi Technologies, USA
GEC-Marconi C3I Ltd
   Command, Control, Communications and Intelligence
   Simulation and Training
   Air Traffic Systems
EASAMS Ltd
MAGEC Aviation Ltd
GEC-Marconi Electronic Systems Corp, USA
Lear Astronics Corp, USA
GEC-Marconi Aerospace Inc, USA
GEC-Marconi Avionics Ltd
GEC-Marconi Aerospace Systems
   Display Systems
   Radar Systems
   Flight Systems
   Power Systems
   Support
   GEC-Marconi Avionics Inc, USA
GEC-Marconi Sensors Ltd
GEC-Marconi Infra-Red Ltd
GEC-Marconi InFlight Systems Ltd
GEC-Marconi Systems Pty Ltd, Australia
Matra Marconi Space NV, Holland (49.0%)
Matra Marconi Space UK Ltd (49.0%)
GEC-Marconi Materials Technology Ltd
GEC-Marconi Materials Corporation, USA
GEC-Marconi Research Centre, Baddow Marconi SpA, Italy
Marconi Automazione SpA, Italy
GEC-Marconi Communication Ltd
Marconi Communications Inc, USA
Marconi Kominikasyon AS, Turkey (51.0%)
Canadian Marconi Company (51.6%)
Cincinnati Electronics Corp, USA (52.35%)
VSEL

Hunting Engineering

The origins of the Hunting organization date back to 1874, the year in which Charles Hunting purchased two sailing ships. Over the years the shipping business developed and today the organization has grown and diversified into many other areas, including oil, aircraft support, shipbroking and defence. In 1995 Hunting plc employs approximately 14,250 people worldwide and has a turnover approaching £1,060 million, making it one of the top 200 Groups in the UK. Hunting plc consists of three Divisions; Defence, Aviation and Oil.

Hunting Plc Defence Division
The Defence Division comprises Hunting Engineering Limited, Irvin Aerospace Limited, Hunting BRAE, and Halmatic Limited, employing approximately 8000 people and having a turnover in the region of £440M.

Hunting Engineering Limited
Hunting Engineering Limited is one of the UK's major defence companies engaged in the development and large scale production - principally as prime contractor - of weapon systems for HM Government and approved overseas customers. In the fiscal year 1994, Hunting Engineering Limited had a turnover of £119 million. Based at Ampthill in Bedfordshire, the Company employees around 1000 people.

For over 30 years Hunting Engineering has been at the forefront of advanced defence technology, responsible for the design, development and production of air force, army and naval weapon systems. These include:

BL755 - the air delivered cluster weapon, sold to 17 nations and cleared for carriage on 22 aircraft.

JP233 - the proven low level airfield attack weapon which dispenses cratering munitions (SG357) and area denial mines (HB876). Delivered by Tornado, JP233 was used to great effect during the Gulf War and is in service with the Royal Air Force and another overseas force.

CHAMPS - a computerised Chinook and Hercules Advanced Mission Planning System now in service with the Royal Air Force.

LAW80 - a light anti-tank weapon in service with the British Army and many other overseas forces.

ARGES - the Company is participating in a tri-national (UK, France, Germany), intelligent off-route, anti-tank mine which is in full development for the three partners' land forces.

MLRS II - Production Prime Contractor for integration of the German AT2 anti-armour mine submunition into the rocket system of MLRS. MLRS II will provide the Company with Production Prime Contractor work to 1995.

Hunting Engineering's specialist capabilities are wide ranging and include: warhead and submunition design and development; dispensing and ejection systems; systems effectiveness studies; software engineering; robotics; information technology and electronics.

Hunting is an acknowledged leader in the field of advanced warhead design and development for the defeat of fixed targets and homogenous and complex armours such as ERA. Extensive work is being undertaken in this area, particularly for US government research agencies.

The company is also involved in dispensing technology for air, land, sea and space applications. Dispensing and ejection technology covers many disciplines including design - incorporating composite materials - aerodynamics, system integration and ejection technologies, using various energy sources and dispensing control, sequencing and safety systems.

International Collaboration
Hunting Engineering's expertise provides an important contribution to many international collaborative programmes including, the Multiple Launch Rocket System (MLRS), where the Company is the UK shareholder in the European Production Group based in Munich, and the European, Autonomous, Off Route Mine programme (ACEATM).

218

The company's policy is one of continuous product improvement. Its current range of submunitions is adaptable for carriage in a variety of weapon dispensers, including stand-off missiles. Continued investment in the design and development of advanced warheads, submunitions and complete weapon systems ensures that the company remains at the forefront of world defence technology.

Future Projects
The Company continues its investment in research and development in order to fulfil the future equipment requirements of the British Armed Services, and of approved overseas governments. In the air systems area, Hunting Engineering will be responding to the Royal Air Force Staff Requirement (Air) 138 as Prime Contactor for the development and production of the Smart Weapon Anti Armour 2000 (SWAARM 2000). The company will also be involved in the Conventionally Armed Stand-off Missile (CASOM) programme to meet the requirement for an air launched missile for the RAF. On the land systems side, Hunting Engineering is developing advanced concepts to fulfil the British Army's requirement for future mines, anti-tank weapons and improved artillery systems.

Communications Division
The Communications Division of Hunting Engineering has been involved in every major Communication and Information Systems (CIS) installation for the British Army and provides a complete design, development and production service for installations and military shelters and field generators. As a member of the Crossbow Consortium, led by ITT Defence, Communications Division has been awarded a multi-million pound development contract within the British Army's Combat Radio Replacement programme - BOWMAN. The Communications Division's involvement in the two-year contract includes: installation design for vehicles, ships and aircraft: radio peripherals design; integrated logistic support and risk management. Using private venture capital, the Communications Division has developed HIWAY, a new fibre optic data distribution system for future CIS installations. A system based upon this technology is now in service with the US Special Forces.

HIWAY is a leading contender for the British Army's VICDS requirement. The Communications Division also has the largest independent electromagnetic assessment facility in Europe, which is located at Pershore in the Midlands. It operates an accredited and NAMAS approved test house which is recognized by CESG for Tempest work. The Division tests all types of equipment in the military and commercial sectors, to appropriate defence and commercial standards, including requirements under the EEC Directive for 1992.

Irvin Aerospace Limited
The Company, which was established over 75 years ago, designs and manufactures a wide range of parachutes, retarders, camouflage, safety and survival systems for defence and aerospace applications. It has sites in England, Italy, Canada and the USA. Its headquarters are located at Hunting Engineering's main site at Ampthill in Bedfordshire.

Irvin manufactures and supports the largest range of parachutes and related equipment in the World. Its products include:

- Personnel parachutes
- Emergency escape parachutes
- Aerial delivery systems
- Missiles/RPV/UAV recovery systems
- Parachutes for use in space exploration
- Ordnance retarders
- Brake parachutes
- Aeromechanical products
- Decoys and Radomes

Hunting-BRAE Limited
This is a joint venture company, 51% owned by Hunting Defence Division with Brown & Root Limited owning 31%, and AEA Technology 18%, set up to manage and operate the Atomic Weapon Establishment (AWE) in an efficient and effective manner. In keeping with the nature and importance of the operation, requirements for safety and security remain paramount. Hunting-BRAE has been involved in the management of AWE under a contract from the Ministry of Defence since Phase I commenced in October 1990. The contract for Phase II, full contractorisation, commenced on 1st April 1993.

The contract duration is seven years. The assets of the establishment will remain in Government ownership with Hunting-BRAE operating them under licence. AWE employees have transferred to the new company, the Atomic Weapons Establishment plc, which is a wholly-owned subsidiary of Hunting- BRAE but in which the MOD retains a "special share."

Halmatic Limited (Hunting Subsidiary)

Halmatic is a wold-renowned boatbuilder and marine services specialist based at Saxon Wharf, near Southampton Water. The company has a well-earned reputation for the manufacture of pilot launches, lifeboats, search and rescue, RIBs, special-purpose workboats, survey vessels, mooring craft, diving support boats, fishing boats and for fisheries patrol and research vessels. The flexibility and variety of Halmatic's range of commercial craft is unsurpassed. For military, law enforcement, defence and resource protection application, Halmatic's pedigree includes patrol boats, police, coastguard and customs launches, fisheries protection vessels and RIBs for special forces.

Working closely with leading-name and in-house designers means that Halmatic hulls, in GRP, steel and aluminium, are recognised as being advanced and of proven quality, dedicated to meeting specific needs.

Halmatic Marine Services is the support service arm of Halmatic Limited, providing, refit, refurbishment and maintenance services to the commercial fleet operator and individual boat owner.

British Aerospace (Bae).

Total British Aerospace sales during 1994 were £7,153 million of which the Defence Division's share was £4,587 million (£412 million profit before interest). The other two major division of the company are Commercial Aerospace and Property. The latest figures suggest that the company employs approximately 80,000 people of whom some 30,000 are in the Defence Division.

During 1994 export markets accounted for 82% of defence sales. However the success in securing UK MoD contracts for the Mid-Life Update of 142 Tornado aircraft, a follow on order for ASRAAM missiles and substantial increases in ammunition orders, probably means that in the short term BAe's domestic market share could show a significant increase.

Air Systems

During 1994 42 x Hawk aircraft were delivered, including the successful introduction of the first of the single seat Series 200 variant on completion of the Company funded development programme.

The Hawk 200 and the other recent addition to the Hawk family, the Hawk 100 Series, are now in service with overseas customers. Deliveries in 1994 included the first Hawk 100 to the Malaysian Air Force early in the year.

The Hawk has now been sold to 14 nations including the UK.

Further training aircraft were ordered by Saudi Arabia following the award in 1993 of contracts for a further new batch of Tornado aircraft. BAe continue to provide a high level of in-Kingdom support to the Royal Saudi Air Force and the Royal Saudi Navy. The new build programme for the 48 Tornado aircraft continued with the first fuselage sub-assembly for the new batch transferred from Samlesbury to the final assembly facility in December 1994 ahead of programme.

The Harrier T10 programme achieved target of seven aircraft delivered to the RAF following first flight in April 1994. The T10 supersedes the long serving Harrier T Mk4. It gives the RAF the additional capabilities of night flight and enhanced weapon system training, and embodies the full operational capability of the single seat GR Mk7.

An important milestone in the Eurofighter 2000 programme was achieved with the flights in Germany and the UK, of the first two development aircraft with the full development programme continuing. All seven development aircraft were structurally completed, engine performance was shown to be well up to expectation and work on the active flight control system and other avionic systems made substantial progress. Recent Eurofighter 2000 activity has focused on programme re-orientation to meet revised customer requirements.

BAe's development programme for the ASRAAM (Advanced Short Range Air to Air Missile) missile, which will form part of the Eurofighter 2000 weapon system, was achieved on target and the first missiles were flown on an F-16 trials aircraft in the USA. Work was also under way on proposals for three further new UK MoD air launched missile programmes: a Conventionally Armed Stand Off Missile (CASOM); an air launched anti-armour weapon drawing on ASRAAM technology; and a next generation advanced medium range air to air missile.

Naval Systems
British Aerospace is a major participant in both the Goshawk T-45 and AV-8B Harrier II+ naval aviation programmes in the USA. Deliveries of Harrier II components to collaborative partner McDonnell Douglas continued to schedule for US, Italian and Spanish aircraft and a contract for remanufactured AV-8B aircraft was placed by the US Marine Corps. The T-45 variant of the Hawk assembled by McDonnell Douglas saw the first batch of students complete flying training. Over 50 T-45 component sets have now been delivered.

In the UK the naval Harrier programme was boosted with an order for a further 18 new-build F/A2 Sea Harrier aircraft and development work on the T4/T8 Sea Harrier trainer upgrade was completed to contract with the first flight in July

BAe is in the process of submitting a bid in 1995 for the Royal Air Force's Replacement Maritime Patrol Aircraft. The company is proposing a complete re-vamp of current RAF Nimrod aircraft, with a major avionics update, as the most cost effective method of fulfilling the RAF's requirement until well into the next century.

British Aerospace joined other US partners in the Joint Advanced Strike Technology (JAST) programme in October 1994 in a US government programme to develop technology for the next generation of combat aircraft, including A-STOVL (Advanced-Short Takeoff Vertical Landing) variants.

An agreement was signed with CMN of France for the integration and marketing of naval guided weapons on the CMN range of naval vessels. The BAeSEMA joint venture achieved a significant success with the award of an initial 36m contract for the Command and Control system for the Korean destroyer programme. The value of the programme to BAeSEMA over some 20 vessels is anticipated to exceed £200m. In January 1995 BAeSEMA was awarded a £40m contract by the UK MoD for the design and build of an Ocean Survey Vessel to enter service with the Royal Navy in 1997. Construction of the ship is being subcontracted to Appledore shipbuilders under the supervision and design authority of BAeSEMA subsidiary YARD.

Land Systems
Deliveries of BAe's Rapier 2000 air defence system continued to the UK MoD and an order was received from Switzerland for an upgrade of their Rapier equipment. Successful development firings were achieved for the Merlin guided mortar round and the medium range Trigat anti-tank missile.

Contained within substantial UK multi-year ammunition purchases were an extension of a small arms ammunition agreement from five to seven years and a 40m mortar bomb order.

Land systems export orders included the award of contract for 105mm Light Guns, ammunition and mortars from Brazil, and the first two of an order for Royal Ordnance Combat Engineer Tractors were delivered for export. British Aerospace Australia involvement in two military vehicle programmes in Australia, the Light Armoured Vehicle and Bushrangers projects, significantly added to the order book in this sector.

British Aerospace was awarded a feasibility contract to lead an international team in a Ballistic Missile Defence study. The study will identify enabling technologies required for this potentially important defence concept.

Subsidiaries

Defence
Arab British Dynamics Co (30%)	Egypt
Asia Pacific Training and Simulation Pte Ltd (63%)	Singapore
BAeSEMA Ltd (50%)	UK
British Aerospace Australia (Holdings) Ltd	Australia
British Aerospace (Canada) Ltd	Canada
British Aerospace Defence Ltd	UK
British Aerospace (Dynamics) Ltd	UK
British Aerospace (Sweden) A	Sweden

British Aerospace (Systems and Equipment) Ltd	UK
Eurofighter Jagdflugzeug GmbH (33%)	Germany
Heckler & Koch GmbH (33%)	Germany
Muiden Chemie International BV	Holland
Nanoquest Defence Products Ltd	UK
Panavia Aircraft GmbH (42.5%)	Germany
Royal Ordnance plc	UK
RWT Ltd	UK
SEPECAT SA (50%)	France
Singapore British Engineering Pte Ltd (40%)	Singapore
Steinheil Optronik GmbH	Germany

Commercial Aerospace

Airbus Finance Company Ltd (20%)	Ireland
Airbus Industrie GIE (20%)	France
Avro International Aerospace Ltd	UK
British Aerospace Airbus Ltd	UK
British Aerospace Regional Aircraft Ltd	UK
British Aerospace (Toulouse) Ltd	UK
Jetstream Aircraft Ltd	UK
Others Arlington Securities Plc	UK
Asia Pacific Space and Communications Inc (44%)	USA
BAe Finance BV	Holland
British Aerospace (Consultancy Services) Ltd	UK
British Aerospace Enterprises Ltd	UK
British Aerospace Flying College Ltd	UK
British Aerospace Holdings, Inc	USA
British Aerospace (Insurance) Ltd	UK
British Aerospace Insurance (Overseas) Ltd	Isle of Man
British Aerospace (International) Ltd	UK
British Aerospace (Investments) Ltd	UK
British Aerospace (Liverpool Airport) Ltd	UK
British Aerospace (Operations) Ltd	UK
British Aerospace (Overseas Holdings) Ltd	UK
British Aerospace Properties Ltd	UK
Hutchinson Telecommunictions (UK) LTd (30%)	UK

International Private Satellite Partnership LP (25%)	UK
Liverpool Airport plc (76%)+	UK
National Remote Sensing Centre Ltd (53%)	UK
Reflectone Inc (53%)	USA
Reflectone UK Ltd (53%)	UK
The Burwood House Group Plc (50%)	UK

Rolls Royce Plc

Rolls-Royce is a high integrity engineering group providing advanced cost-effective technology to aerospace and industrial power systems markets world wide. It probably fair to say that Rolls-Royce is a world leader in its chosen product fields: aero, marine and industrial gas turbines, power generation, nuclear engineering and materials handling.

Rolls-Royce operates through two main units: the Aerospace Group, specialising in gas turbines for civil and military aircraft; and the Industrial Power Group which designs, constructs and installs complete power generation, transmission and distribution systems and major equipment for marine propulsion, oil and gas pumping, offshore and defence markets.

In 1994 more than 70 per cent of the company's sales were achieved overseas. Group turnover in 1994 was as follows:

| Aerospace Group | £1,962 million |
| Industrial Power Group | £1,201 million |

Aerospace Group operations

Rolls-Royce Military Aero Engines Limited

Reduced levels of defence spending worldwide have continued to affect the company's military engines sales, but, overall, the business performance was satisfactory, with a steady development and production workload.

Rolls Royce's product base covers engines for combat and trainer aircraft and helicopter markets. In 1995, RB199 engine production recommences for the Royal Saudi Air Force and the company remains involved in Europe's two new helicopter engine projects. The MTR390 engine continued flight trials for its initial application, the Franco-German Tiger. The RTM322 engine accumulated flight test hours in the EH101, orders for which have recently been announced by the UK MoD.

The Italian navy took delivery of the first of its single-seat Pegasus-powered harrier aircraft in October. The Pegasus is now in service aboard the aircraft carriers of four navies in addition to service with the US Marine Corps and the Royal Air Force.

A new Polish trainer, the Viper-powered Iryda M-93V, made its international debut at Farnborough 94 and is undertaking flight certification.

Rolls-Royce Aero Engine Services Limited
In 1994 the mix of engine maintenance activity continued to change away from work for the Ministry of Defence and towards the provision of overhaul services for commercial customers, most of whom are based abroad.

There was a dramatic growth in the order book as the company's investment in back up service, quality and improved management began to pay off and customers recognised the benefit of longer term contracts. Customers in the USA, China, Switzerland, Korea, Cyprus and the United Kingdom have all signed long-term contracts with Rolls Royce.

The entry into service of new civil engines with operators who have not been traditional customers has allowed the company to further broaden their customer base. Several major airlines still perform engine overhaul work for themselves but, in 1994, a growing number turned to Rolls Royce for maintenance programmes or the specialist refurbishment of individual parts.

Five new long-term contracts were announced at the beginning of 1995: for RB211 work from Britannia Airways, Air 2000 and American Tans Air, V2500 maintenance and Airtours, and Tay overhauls from China.

New orders were dominated by the Tay and RB211-535E4 engines, with their reliability and economy continuing to prove a significant attraction in short and

227

medium haul markets. Powering the successful Fokker 70/100 range, the Tay won new orders from Air Inter, Air Littoral, Malev, Silk Air and Tyrolean.

The 535E4 reinforced its market dominance. Rolls Royce received new orders from American Trans Air and four customers from former Soviet republics.

An RB211-524B4 of Delta Air Lines established a new world record of 27,532 hours on-wing - equivalent to more than three years non-stop flying.

The Trent 700 engine completed flight certification in the A330 including clearance for long over-water flights. The engine was selected by Dragonair and has entered commercial service with Cathay Pacific. The larger Trent 800 was chosen for the Boeing 777 by Transbrasil in 1994.

Amongst the collaborative engine programmes, the International Aero Engines V2500, continued development and received new orders - notably from China and the United States.

The BMW Rolls-Royce BR715 was selected as sole powerplant for the new MD-95 airliner. Meanwhile, Gulfstream, whose GV aircraft will fly with the first BR710 engines later this year, made the decision to continue production of the GIV and GV in parallel and, late in 1994, placed an order for a further batch of Tays for the GIV.

Industrial Power Group operations
In the power generation, transmission and distribution markets demand is increasingly for complete systems, rather than individual products or sub-systems. Rolls Royce's project management teams are capable of managing the most complex turnkey projects and can draw on the wide range of skills and experience available in their specialist companies to meet a customer's precise needs.

Rolls-Royce Power Engineering plc
Parsons Power Generation Systems successfully concluded negotiations for a 208MW gas-fired combined cycle power station at Kakinada, in India, worth 150 million and another £60 million contract to build a 60MW power station at Samarinda in Indonesia.

Rolls-Royce Industrial & Marine Gas Turbines Limited
Three of the major new product development programmes being undertaken by Rolls-Royce are being managed by this company. These are: the development of an industrial version of the Trent 800 aero engine; the WR-21 intercooled recuperative naval propulsion system for the US Navy; the dry low emissions combustion technology, initially for the Industrial RB211 but for future application to all Rolls-Royce aero-derived industrial gas turbines.

Cooper Rolls, the joint venture between Rolls-Royce and Cooper Industries Inc., maintained its major share in the oil and gas market in 1994. Substantial orders were obtained from operators in Thailand, Canada and the North Sea.

Roll-Royce Nuclear Engineering Limited
The first of a new generation of long-life cores developed by Rolls-Royce & Associates for Royal Navy nuclear submarines, moved into the manufacturing stage. These new core are designed to last the lifetme of a nuclear submarine, eliminating the need for costly reactor refuelling.

Nuclear Plant Services obtained a five-year maintenance contract from Nuclear Electric for the Bradwell Magnox power station. This contract is the first of its sort awarded by Nuclear Electric and represents a significant recognition of Rolls Royce's ability to handle complex outage arrangements.

The first two elements of the Thompson Defence Projects bridging contract for the British Army were formally accepted for service. The close support and general support bridges are part of the Bridging for the 1990s system being developed unde a £140 million contract won in 1993.

Rolls Royce Industries Canada Inc
Rolls-Royce Canada, a repair and overhaul base in Montreal, enjoyed a successful year in an extremely demanding market-place. Highlights of 1994 included a number of significant contracts, including three for different Mexican airlines.

Bristol Aerospace were adversely affected by the significant reductions in

Canada's defence programmes during 1994. However the company concluded an agreement with Northrop Grumman to offer upgrades on F-5 aircraft worldwide and also won a contract to carry out work on F-5 wings for the Norwegian Air Force.

PRINCIPAL SUBSIDIARY UNDERTAKINGS

Incorporated overseas

Aerospace Group

Motores Rolls-Royce Limitada	Brazil
Rolls-Royce Technical Support SARL	France

Industrial Power Group

Rolls-Royce Industrial Power (Pacific) Limited	Australia
Bristol Aerospace Limited	Canada
Ferranti-Packard Transformers Limited	Canada
Parsons Turbine Generators Canada Limited	Canada
Rolls-Royce Canada Limited	Canada
Rolls-Royce Gas Turbine Engines (Canada) Ltd	Canada
Rolls-Royce Holdings Canada Inc.	Canada
Rolls-Royce Industries Canada Inc.	Canada
Ferranti-Packard de Mexico SA De CV	Mexico
Rolls-Royce Industrial Power (New Zealand) Limited	New Zealand
NEI Africa Holdings Limited (60.33%)	South Africa
Northern Engineering Industries Africa Limited (56.36%)	South Africa
Cutler Hammer Zambia Limited	Zambia
NEI Zambia Limited	Canada
NEI Holdings Zimbabwe (Private) Limited	Zimbabwe

Corporate

Rolls-Royce of Australia Pty. Limited	Australia
Nightingale Insurance Limited	Guernsey
RR International Turbines (Saudi Arabia) Limited (51%)	Saudi Arabia
Rolls-Royce Holdings Inc.	USA
Rolls-Royce Inc.	USA
Rolls-Royce Capital Inc.	US

PRINCIPAL ASSOCIATED UNDERTAKINGS

Registered in England or Scotland
Aerospace Group
Rolls-Royce Turbomeca Limited (England & France)
Rolls Smiths Engine Controls Limited
RS Leasing Limited
Turbo-Union Limited (England, Germany & Italy)

Industrial Power Group
Rolls Wood Group (Repair & Overhauls) Limited
Cooper Rolls Limited
Rolls Laval heat Exchangers Limited

Corporate
Rolls-Royce & Partners Finance Limited

Incorporated Overseas

Aerospace group

BMW Rolls-Royce GmbH (UK & Germany)	Germany
EUROJET Turbo GmbH (UK, Germany, Italy & Spain)	Germany
MTU, Turbomeca, Rolls-Royce GmbH (UK, France & Germany)	Germany
Industria de Turbo Propulsores SA	Spain
IAE Aero Engines AG (UK, Germany, Italy, Japan & USA)	Switzerland
Williams-Rolls, Inc. (Europe & North America)	USA
Cooper, Rolls Corporation	Canada
Belliss India Limited	India
Easun Reyrolle Relays and Devices Limited	India
Cooper Rolls Incorporated (Europe & North America)	USA

Corporate

Middle East propulsion Company Limited	Saudi Arabia
R-H Component Technologies, L.C.	USA

PART 6 - MISCELLANEOUS

The Services Hierarchy

Officer Ranks

Army	Navy	RAF
Field Marshal	Admiral of the Fleet	Marshal of the Royal Air Force
General	Admiral	Air Chief Marshal
Lieutenant-General	Vice-Admiral	Air Marshal
Major General	Rear-Admiral	Air Vice Marshal
Brigadier	Commodore	Air Commodore
Colonel	Captain	Group Captain
Lieutenant-Colonel	Commander	Wing Commander
Major	Lieutenant-Commander	Squadron Leader
Captain	Lieutenant	Flight-Lieutenant
Lieutenant	Sub-Lieutenant	Flying Officer
Second Lieutenant	Midshipman	Pilot Officer

Non Commissioned Ranks

Army	RAF	NAVY
Warrant Officer 1/2	Warrant Officer	Warrant Officer
Staff/Colour Sergeant	Flight Sergeant	Chief Petty Officer
Sergeant	Sergeant	Petty Officer
Corporal	Corporal	Leading Rate
Lance Corporal	Senior Aircraftman	Able Rate
Private	Leading Aircraftman	Ordinary Rate
	Aircraftman	

Note: In general terms the rank shown in each column equates to the other service ranks shown alongside.

Pay Scales (1 April 1995)

The following are a selection from the Army Pay scales relevant from 1 April 1995. Approximate scales for the other two services can be identified by using the previous table of commissioned and non-commissioned ranks. Pay scales apply to both males and females

Officers	On Appointment	Rising To
University Cadet	7,635	10,741
Second Lieutenant	13,315	-
Lieutenant	17,600	19,454
Captain	22,509	26,166
Major	28,564	34,229
Lieutenant Colonel	40,270	44,504
Colonel	46,891	51,826
Brigadier	57,578	

Notes:
(1) Rates of pay apply to both male and female officers.
(2) QARANC Officers are commissioned as Lieutenants.

The following rates apply to non-commissioned officers and soldiers and are a selection showing some of the most common rates. From the 1st January 1991 all recruits have been enlisted on an Open Engagement for a period of 22 years service from the age of 18 or the date of enlistment whichever is the later. Subject to giving 12 months notice, and any time bar that may be in force, all service personnel have the right to leave on the completion of 3 years reckonable service from the age of 18.

Adult Soldiers	Band	Scale A (£ per week)	per Annum
Private Class 4	1	159.88	8,336
Private Class 1	1	217.84	11,358
Private Class 1	3	278.81	14,537
Lance Corporal Class 1	1	250.32	13,052
Lance Corporal Class 1	3	314.02	16,373

Corporal Class 1	1	288.54	15,045
Corporal Class 1	3	352.24	18,366
Sergeant	5	350.28	18,264
Staff Sergeant	5	368.48	19,213
Warrant Officer Class 2	6	434.63	22,662
Warrant Officer Class 1	7	501.69	26,159

Aircraft Accidents 1 Jan 1994 - 31 Dec 1994

Date	Aircraft	Service	Killed	Serious Injury
05 Jan	Sea Harrier	RN	-	-
14 Jan	Harrier	RAF	1	-
23 Feb	Lynx	RN	-	-
25 Mar	Lynx	RN	-	-
25 Mar	Sea King	RN	-	1
10 Apr	Lynx	AAC	-	-
16 Apr	Sea Harrier	RN	-	-
05 May	VC-10	RAF	-	1
20 May	Tornado	RAF	-	1
02 Jun	Chinook	RAF	29	-
07 Jun	Tornado	RAF	-	-
08 Jul	Tornado	RAF	2	-
19 Jul	Tornado	RAF	-	-
23 Jul	Lynx	AAC	-	-
30 Jul	Nimrod	RAF	-	1
01 Aug	Tornado	RAF	-	-
04 Aug	Hercules	RAF	1	-
01 Sep	Tornado	RAF	2	-
05 Sep	Lynx	RN	-	1
19 Sep	Tornado	RAF	-	-
22 Sep	Lynx	AAC	2	-
12 Oct	Sea King	RN	-	1
11 Nov	Gazelle	AAC	-	1
15 Dec	Sea Harrier	RN	-	-

ARRC Groupings (By Divisions)

Composition of the 7th German Panzer Division

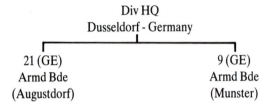

Div HQ
Dusseldorf - Germany

| 21 (GE) Armd Bde (Augustdorf) | 9 (GE) Armd Bde (Munster) |

Composition of the Multinational Division (Central) - MND(C)

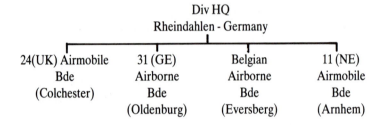

Div HQ
Rheindahlen - Germany

| 24(UK) Airmobile Bde (Colchester) | 31 (GE) Airborne Bde (Oldenburg) | Belgian Airborne Bde (Eversberg) | 11 (NE) Airmobile Bde (Arnhem) |

Composition of the Multinational Division (South) - MND(S)

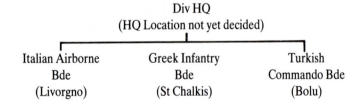

Div HQ
(HQ Location not yet decided)

| Italian Airborne Bde (Livorgno) | Greek Infantry Bde (St Chalkis) | Turkish Commando Bde (Bolu) |

Composition of the 1st (UK) Armoured Division

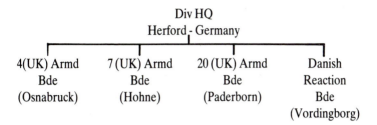

Div HQ
Herford - Germany

| 4(UK) Armd Bde (Osnabruck) | 7 (UK) Armd Bde (Hohne) | 20 (UK) Armd Bde (Paderborn) | Danish Reaction Bde (Vordingborg) |

Composition of the 3rd (UK) Mechanised Division

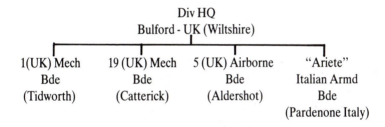

Div HQ
Bulford - UK (Wiltshire)

| 1(UK) Mech Bde (Tidworth) | 19 (UK) Mech Bde (Catterick) | 5 (UK) Airborne Bde (Aldershot) | "Ariete" Italian Armd Bde (Pardenone Italy) |

Composition of the 3rd Italian Mechanised Division

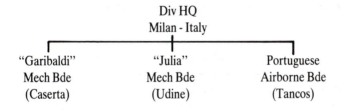

Div HQ
Milan - Italy

| "Garibaldi" Mech Bde (Caserta) | "Julia" Mech Bde (Udine) | Portuguese Airborne Bde (Tancos) |

Composition of the 2nd Greek Mechanised Division

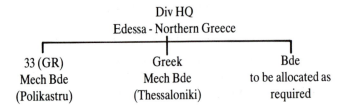

Div HQ
Edessa - Northern Greece

33 (GR)	Greek	Bde
Mech Bde	Mech Bde	to be allocated as
(Polikastru)	(Thessaloniki)	required

Note: Other NATO nations could be invited to contribute a similar brigade to act as the third brigade within this divisional framework structure.

Composition of the 1st United States Armoured Division

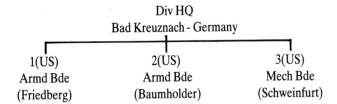

Div HQ
Bad Kreuznach - Germany

1(US)	2(US)	3(US)
Armd Bde	Armd Bde	Mech Bde
(Friedberg)	(Baumholder)	(Schweinfurt)

Composition of the 1st Turkish Mechanised Division

Div HQ
Ankara - Turkey

23 (TU)	Turkish	Bde
Mech Bde	Armd Bde	to be allocated as
(Ankara)	(Karikkale)	required

Composition of the Spanish FAR Contingent

(Fuerza De Accion Rapida) HQ
Madrid - Spain

| Airborne Bde (Madrid) | Spanish Legion Inf Bde (Malaga) | Mountain Brigade (Huesca) | Helicopter Transport Regt (Madrid) |

Note: The Spanish FAR equates roughly to the size of a conventional division.

Quotations For 1996-97

"The beatings will continue until morale improves"
Attributed to the Commander of the Japanese Submarine Force

"Hell hath no fury like a non-combatant"
Charles Montague 1867-1928

"The Navy is very old and very wise"
Rudyard Kipling "The Fringes of the Fleet" 1915

"During WWII the US Army concluded that almost every soldier, if he had escaped death or wounds, would break down after 200-240 "combat days". The British who rotated their troops out of the front line more often, reckoned 400 days, but they agreed that breakdown was inevitable. The reason that only one sixth of the casualties was psychiatric was that most combat troops did not survive long enough to go to pieces
Gwyn Dyer - 1986

"It takes the Royal Navy about three years to build a ship. It would take about three hundred years to rebuild a tradition"

Admiral Sir Andrew Browne Cunningham resisting plans for the Royal Navy to abandon soldiers stranded in Crete during May 1941

"You know" Colonel Summers told a Vietnamese colonel after the war "You never defeated us on the battlefield". To which his communist conterpart replied "That may be so but it is irrelevant"

Stanley Karnow - Vietnam: A History 1983

"My solution to the problem would be to tell the Viet Cong they've got to draw in their horns and stop their aggression or we're going to bomb them back into the Stone Age"

US Air Force General Curtis LeMay - 1965

Walking into the hotel (in Port Stanley) was the fulfilment of a dream, a fantasy that had filled all our thoughts for almost three months. " We never doubted for a moment that the British would come," said the proprietor, Desmond King. "We have just been waiting for the moment".

Max Hastings - Press Despatch from the Falkland Islands June 1982

We could not resist:

"The batsman is my shepherd, I shall not crash,
He makes me to land on flat runways
He bringeth me off in rough waters.
He restoreth my confidence.
Yea, though I come stalling into the deck at sixty knots
I shall fear no evil,
For he is with me
His arms and his bats comfort me.
He prepareth a deck before me in the presence of mine enemies.
He attacheth my hook to the wire.
My deck space runneth over.

The Batsman - Anon - Fleet Air Arm - 1950s

Abbreviations

The following is a selection from the list of standard NATO abbreviations and should assist users of this handbook.

A&AEE	Aeroplane & Armament Experimental Establishment
AAC	Army Air Corps
AAM	Air to Air Missile
AAR	Air to Air Refueling
AB	Able Seaman
ac	Aircraft
ACCGS	Air Cadets Central Gliding School
accn	Accommodation
ACE	Allied Command Europe
AD	Air Defence/Air Dispatch/Army Department
ADA	Air Defended Area
Adjt	Adjutant
admin	Administration
admin O	Administrative Order
ADOC	Air Defence Operations Centre
ADP	Automatic Data Processing
ADR	Airfield Damage Repair
ADV	Air Defence Variant
AEF	Air Experience Flight
AEW	Airborne Early Warning
AFCENT	Allied Forces Central European Theatre
Airmob	Airmobile
ALARM	Air Launched Anti Radiation Missile
ALM	Air Loadmaster
amn	airman
AMRAAM	Advanced Medium Range Air to Air Missile
AOC	Air Officer Commanding
ARRF	Allied Rapid Reaction Forces
ASRAAM	Advanced Short Range Air to Air Missile
ATAF	Allied Tactical Air Force
ATC	Air Traffic Control; Air Training Corps

Atk	Antitank
armr	Armour
armd	Armoured
AFV	Armoured Fighting Vehicle
AMF(L)	Allied Mobile Force (Land Element)
AMP	Air Member for Personnel
APC	Armoured Personnel Carrier
APDS	Armour Piercing Discarding Sabot
AP	Armour Piercing/Ammunition Point/Air Publication
ARRC	Allied Rapid Reaction Corps
ASF	Aircraft Servicing Flight
ATGW	Anti Tank Guided Weapon
att	Attached
AWOL	Absent Without Official Leave
BAe	British Aerospace
BALTAP	Baltic Approaches
BE	Belgium (Belgian)
BMEWS	Ballistic Missile Early Warning System
bde	Brigade
BAOR	British Army of the Rhine
BFG	British Forces Germany
BFPO	British Forces Post Office
BRSC	British Rear Support Command
cam	Camouflaged
cas	Casualty
CASEVAC	Casualty Evacuation
cat	Catering
CAD	Cental Ammunition Depot
CAP	Combat Air Patrol
CATCS	Central Air Traffic Control School
CCTV	Closed Circuit Television
Cdo	Commando
CEP	Circular Error Probable
CEPS	Central European Pipeline System
CET	Combat Engineer Tractor
C-in-C	Commander in Chief

CINCENT	Commander in Chief Central European Theatre
CFE	Conventionl Forces Europe
CFS	Central Flying School
CGRM	Commandant General Royal Marines
Ch	Challenger
COC	Combat Operations Centre
CoS	Chief of Staff
CPO	Chief Petty Officer
CRC	Control & Reporting Centre
CRP	Control & Reporting Post
CVD	Central Vehicle Depot
CW	Chemical Warfare
civ	Civilian
CP	Close Protection/Command Post
c sups	Combat Supplies
comd	Command/Commander
CinC	Commander in Chief
CPO	Command Pay Office/Chief Petty Officer
CO	Commanding Officer
comp rat	Composite Ration (Compo)
COMRFA	Commander Royal Fleet Auxiliary
COMSEN	Communications Centre
coord	Co-ordinate
CCM	Counter Counter Measure
CTTO	Central Trials and Tactics Organisation
DAW	Department of Air Warfare
DCF	Deputy Commander Fleet
DF	Defensive Fire
DIOT	Director of Initial Officer Training (Cranwell)
DK	Denmark
dml	Demolition
det	Detached
div	Division
DRA	Defence Research Agency
DROPS	Demountable Rack off Loading & Pick Up System
DTG	Date Time Group

DS	Direct Support/Dressing Station
DSGT	Department of Specialist Ground Training
ech	Echelon
ECM	Electronic Counter Measure
ECCM	Electronic Counter Counter Measure
EFA	European Fighter Aircraft
EFTS	Elementary Flying Training Squadron
ELINT	Electronic Intelligence
emb	Embarkation
EDP	Emergency Defence Plan
EMP	Electro Magnetic Pulse
en	Enemy
engr	Engineer
EOD	Explosive Ordnance Disposal
eqpt	Equipment
ETA	Estimated Time of Arrival
ETPS	Empire Test Pilots School
EW	Early Warning/Electronic Warfare
EWOSE	Electronic Warfare Operational Support Establishment
ex	Exercise
FGA	Fighter Ground Attack
fmn	Formation
FAC	Forward Air Controller
FEBA	Forward Edge of the Battle Area
FLA	Future Large Aircraft
FLET	Forward Location Enemy Troops
FLIR	Forward Looking Infra Red
FLOT	Forward Location Own Troops
FO	Flag Officer
FONA	Flag Officer Naval Aviation
FOO	Forward Observation Officer
FOSF	Flag Officer Surface Fleet
FOST	Flag Officer Sea Training
FOSM	Flag Officer Submarines
FR	France (French)
FRT	Forward Repair Team

FTS	Flying Training School
FY	Financial Year
GDP	General Defence Plan
GE	German (Germany)
GEF	Ground Equipment Flight
GR	Greece (Greek)
GOC	General Officer Commanding
GPMG	General Purpose Machine Gun
HAS	Hardened Aircraft Shelter
hel	Helicopter
HE	High Explosive
HEAT	High Explosive Anti Tank
HESH	High Explosive Squash Head
HVM	Hyper Velocity Missile
Hy	Heavy
IAM	Institute of Aviation Medicine
IFF	Identification Friend or Foe
IGB	Inner German Border
illum	illuminating
int	Intelligence
IO	Intelligence Officer
INTSUM	Itelligence Summary
IRG	Immediate Replenishment Group
IS	Internal Security
IT	Italy (Italian)
IUKADGE	Improved UK Air Defence Ground Environment
IW	Individual Weapon
JHQ	Joint Headquarters
JSSU	Joint Services Signals Unit
LC	Logistics Command
LGB	Laser Guided Bomb
L of C	Lines of Communication
LLAD	Low Level Air Defence
LO	Liaison Officer
Loc	Locating
log	Logistic

LRATGW	Long Range Anti Tank Guided Weapon
LSW	Light Support Weapon
MAOT	Mobile Air Operations Team
maint	Maintain
mat	Material
med	Medical
MNAD	Multi National Airmobile Division
MND	Multi National Division
MO	Medical Officer
MP	Military Police
MoD	Ministry of Defence
mob	Mobilisation
Mov O	Movement Order
MPA	Mount Pleasant Airfield
MR	Maritime Reconnaissance
MRR	Maritime Radar Reconnaissance
MSAM	Medium Range Surface to Air Missile
msl	missile
MV	Military Vigilance
NAAFI	Navy, Army and Air Force Institutes
NADGE	NATO Air Defence Ground Environment
NATO	North Atlantic Treaty Organisation
NBC	Nuclear Biological and Chemical
NCO	Non Commissioned Officer
nec	Necessary
NL	Netherlands
NO	Norway (Norwegian)
NOK	Next of Kin
ni	Night
NORTHAG	Northern Army Group
NTR	Nothing to Report
NYK	Not Yet Known
OP	Observation Post
OC	Officer Commanding
OCU	Operational Conversion Unit
OEU	Operational Evaluation Unit

OIC	Officer in Charge
OLF	Operational Low Flying
opO	Operation Order
ORB	Omni Radio Beacon
ORBAT	Order of Battle
pax	Passengers
POL	Petrol, Oil and Lubricants
P info	Public Information
PMRAFNS	Princess Mary's Royal Air Force Nursing Service
PO	Portugal (Portuguese)/Petty Officer
PR	Public Relations
PRU	Photographic Recnnaissance Unit
PTC	Pesonnel & Training Command
QCS	Queen's Colour Squadron
QM	Quartermaster
QRA	Quick Reaction Alert
RAP	Rocket Assisted Projectile/Regimental Aid Post
RAuxAF	Royal Auxiliary Air Force
RIC	Reconnaissance Interpretation Centre
RM	Royal Marines
RN	Royal Navy
RP	Reporting Post
RPV	Remotely Piloted Vehicle
RSME	Royal School of Military Engineering
RTM	Ready to Move
R&D	Research and Development
rebro	Rebroadcast
recce	Reconnaissance
RFA	Royal Fleet Auxiliary
rft	Reinforcement
RTU	Return to Unit
SACEUR	Supreme Allied Commander Europe
SAM	Surface to Air Missile
SATCO	Senior Air Traffic Control Officer
SARTU	Search & Rescue Training Unit
2IC	Second in Command

SH	Support Helicopters
SHAPE	Supreme Headquarters Allied Powers Europe
SKTU	Sea King Training Unit
sit	Situation
SITREP	Situation Report
smk	Smoke
SMO	Senior Medical Officer
SNCO	Senior Non Commisioned Officer
SOC	Sector Operations Centre
SP	Spain (Spanish)
Sqn	Squadron
SSM	Surface to Surface Missile
SSR	Secondary Surveillance Radar
SSVC	Services Sound and Vision Corporation
STC	Strike Command
STOL	Short Take Off and Landing
tac	Tactical
TASM	Tactical Air to Surface Missile
tgt	Target
THAAD	Theatre High Altitude Area Defence
TOT	Time on Target
TOW	Tube Launched Optically Tracked Wire Guided Missile
tpt	Transport
TTTE	Tri-National Tornado Training Establishment
TU	Turkish (Turkey)
TWCU	Tornado Weapons Conversion Unit
UAS	University Air Squadron
UK	United Kingdom
UKADGE	United Kingdom Air Defence Ground Environment
UKADR	United Kingdom Air Defence Region
UKRADOC	United Kingdom Region Air Defence Operations Centre
UKLF	United Kingdom Land Forces
UKMF	United Kingdom Mobile Force
UNCLASS	Unclassified
UNFICYP	United Nations Force in Cyprus
UXB	Unexploded Bomb

US	United States
USAF	United States Air Force
veh	Vehicle
VGS	Volunteer Gliding School
VOR	Vehicle off the Road
WE	War Establishment
wh	Wheeled
WIMP	Whinging Incompetent Malingering Person
WMR	War Maintenance Reserve
WO	Warrant Officer
WRNS	Womens Royal Naval Service
WRAC	Womens Royal Army Corps
WRAF	Womens Royal Air Force
wksp	Workshop
X	Crossing (as in roads or rivers)

This publication was produced by R&F (Defence) Publications
Editorial Office 01743-235079

The other publications in this series are:

The Royal Air Force Pocket Guide 1994-95
The British Army Pocket Guide 1995-96

Further copies can be obtained from :

Pen & Sword Books Ltd
47 Church Sreet
Barnsley S70 2AS

Telephone: 01226-734222 Fax: 01226-734438

There are special rates for purchases of more than 10 books.